ב"ה

Thank you for celebra

Family and friends are the light of our lives!

בת מצוה של מרים חיה פדר

כ"ו כסלו תשע"א

Miriam Feder's Bat Mitzvah

December 2nd, 2010

שערי אורה

כי אתה נרי

FLAMES

שערי אורה
כי אתה נרי

FLAMES

a chasidic discourse
from *Gates of Radiance* by
Rabbi DovBer
זצוקללה"ה נבג"מ זי"ע
of Lubavitch

•

translated by
Dr. Naftali Loewenthal

Kehot Publication Society
770 Eastern Parkway / Brooklyn, New York 11213

FLAMES

Second Printing 2004
by
KEHOT PUBLICATION SOCIETY
770 Eastern Parkway / Brooklyn, New York 11213
(718) 774-4000 / Fax (718) 774-2718

Orders:
291 Kingston Avenue / Brooklyn, New York 11213
(718) 778-0226 / Fax (718) 778-4148
www.kehotonline.com

ISBN 0-8266-0464-1

Manufactured in the United States of America

CONTENTS

ב"ה

PREFACE

When Rabbi DovBer, the Mitteler Rebbe, would say Chasidut, there was a perfect hush. Still he would intersperse the Chasidut with, "Sha, sha!"

This was to still the rushing of his intellect...
—Hayom Yom, 4 Adar Sheini

The discourse presented here, beginning with the words *Ki Atah Neiri,* was originally published by the Mitteler Rebbe in his book *Shaarei Orah* ("Gates of Radiance") in 5582 (1882). The present bi-lingual edition of the discourse, entitled *Flames,* marks a milestone in the dissemination of Chasidut, presenting for the very first time a fully user-friendly, English text of Rabbi DovBer's expansive work. This is the sixth volume of the popular *Chasidic Heritage Series.*

Like the powerful torrents of a surging river—such was the manner in which Chasidut flowed through the mind of Rabbi DovBer. One needs only to look at the sheer length of his discourses to recognize that his was a unique style, differing greatly from that of his father, Rabbi Schneur Zalman of Liadi. For while Rabbi Schneur Zalman provided the seminal ideas for the Chabad-Chasidut philosophy, Rabbi DovBer developed and expanded these concepts, adding tremendous width and breadth to his father's doctrine. Indeed, an idea that Rabbi Schneur Zalman explained in one page would often be expounded and articulated by Rabbi DovBer over twenty or thirty pages.

Rabbi Naftoli Loewenthal meticulously prepared the translation of the discourse, and Rabbi Avraham D. Vaisfiche added extensive annotation and commentary to the manuscript. The Hebrew text of the discourse has been re-typeset with Hebrew vowel marks to further enhance this volume's usability. A brief biography of the author's life, prepared by Rabbi Yosef Marcus, has been added as an appendix.

Special thanks are due to Rabbis Yosef B. Friedman, Dovid Olidort and Ari Sollish for their editorial assistance.

Kehot Publication Society

9 Kislev 5763
Birthday and *yahrzeit* of Rabbi DovBer

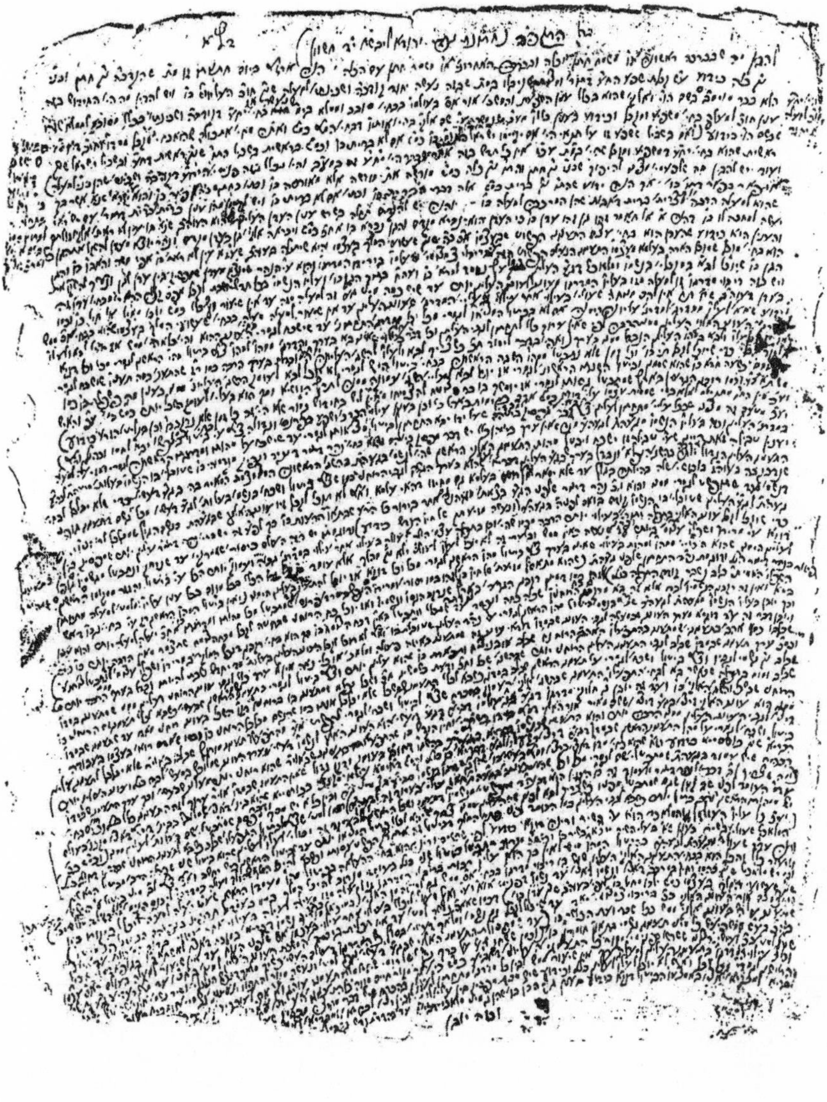

Facsimile of handwritten manuscript by Rabbi DovBer

INTRODUCTION

INTRODUCTION

"The lamp of the Divine is the soul of a man"
—Proverbs 20:27

"For the body of man is a wick, and the light is kindled above it..."
—Zohar III:187a; Tanya ch. 35

The *maamar* by Rabbi DovBer, the second Rebbe of Chabad-Lubavitch, presented here is based on a passage in his father Rabbi Schneur Zalman of Liadi's *Likkutei Amarim Tanya*. The central theme of *Tanya*, as the author states on the title page, is the verse "For it [Torah observance] is very close to you, in your mouth and in your heart, to do it."[1] *Tanya*, called the "Written Torah" of Chabad-Lubavitch teachings, presents an exposition of the concepts of the animal soul, the divine soul, their struggle within the person and the goal that the divine soul should be expressed through the thought, speech and action of the person, by observance of the Torah and its commands. In Chapter 35 the author returns to the theme verse *for it is very close to you* and states that he intends to clarify the final word[2]: "to do it." This means the significance of *action*, the physical performance of the *mitzvot*.

In order to explain this, Rabbi Schneur Zalman quotes a famous passage in the *Zohar*[3] expounded by the *yenuka* ('child'), the prodigious son of Rav Hamnuna, who taught mystical ideas to the Sages of the *Zohar*. This teaching employs the image of an oil lamp to explain the nature of the Jew. The person is the wick, and the flame expresses the radiance of the *Shechinah*,[4] aflame above the person's

1. Deuteronomy 30:14.

2. One word in Hebrew: *la'asoto*.

3. *Zohar* III:187a.

4. SHECHINAH, Divine Presence, is the

head.[5] In order for the flame to burn there must be *oil*: actual good deeds, *mitzvot*.

Rabbi Schneur Zalman's *Tanya* was printed in Kislev 5557 (1796). Some years later on Shabbat during Chanukah 5568 (1807) he delivered a *maamar*,[6] beginning with the verse *For You, G-d, are my Lamp, and G-d will illuminate my darkness*,[7] which develops further the image of the lamp, the wick and the flame. It is thought that Rabbi DovBer, Rabbi Schneur Zalman's oldest son, wrote a transcript of this *maamar*.[8] Later in 5573 (1812), Rabbi DovBer himself became Rebbe, succeeding his father, and was known as the *Mitteler Rebbe*. At some point he wrote a longer version of this *maamar*, and included it in his book *Shaarei Orah* ("Gates of Radiance") published in 5582 (1822), a work in two sections, "Gate of Chanukah" and "Gate of Purim." In each section there are a number of quite lengthy *maamarim*. The *maamar* presented here is one of the shortest.

This *maamar* also begins with the verse *For You, G-d, are my Lamp*. It focuses on the multiple images of the lamp, the wick, the oil and the different colors of the flame in order to express profound guidance in service of G-d for every individual. It can be understood as a discourse specifically about *Chanukah*, and at the same time it is a perennial teaching about serving G-d.

Rabbi DovBer wrote and had published in his life-time a considerable number of books. His grandson Rabbi Shmuel Schneersohn, the fourth Lubavitcher Rebbe, said that some of

---

immanent category of the Divine influence, brought down to earth by the study of the Torah and the practice of mitzvot.

5. The image of radiance shining above a person's head is also found in the Talmud, regarding the repentant Nathan of Tzutzita (*Shabbat* 56b, see *Tosafot*).

6. *Torah Or, Miketz*, 40b.

7. II Samuel 22:29.

8. This is printed in *Maamarei Admur Hazaken 5568*, vol. 2. p. 643. There is another transcript of this *maamar* in the handwriting of Rabbi Menachem Mendel, the Tzemach Tzedek. See his *Or HaTorah*, Chanukah, p. 638, and the comments by the editors of *Torah Or* (Ed. 5751), p. 324. The latter transcript is the basis of the version printed in *Torah Or*.

these were written for specific types of followers: for various kinds of intellectual scholars of Chasidut—called *maskil*—and for the different varieties of people who serve G-d with great depth of heart—called *oved.* However, Rabbi Shmuel continued, two of Rabbi DovBer's books were written for all the Chasidim: *Shaar Hayichud,* "Gate of Unity," which is *the key to Chasidic teachings* and *Shaarei Orah,* "Gates of Radiance," *the Alef Bet of Chasidic teachings.*[9]

To make *Gates of Radiance* more accessible, despite the length of the *maamarim,* Rabbi Yosef Yitzchak of Lubavitch, wrote *Book of Summaries (Sefer Hakitzurim).* This presents relatively brief summaries of each chapter in the book, and also serves as an explanatory commentary. The current Hebrew editions include both Rabbi DovBer's *Gates of Radiance* and Rabbi Yosef Yitzchak's *Book of Summaries,* as well as a subject index compiled by the Rebbe, Rabbi Menachem Mendel Schneerson.

The present publication of the *maamar* beginning *For You, G-d are my Lamp,* has been divided into two parts. Part one comprises chapters 1-10 and part two chapters 11-19. The two parts focus on two complementary themes, both using the image of the lamp. The first part elaborates on the meaning of the first half of the verse, *For You, G-d, are my Lamp* and the second focuses on the second half: *and G-d will illuminate my darkness.*

The theme of the first ten chapters of the *maamar* is the balance between different aspects of spirituality, and in particular the importance of the actual performance of the *mitzvot* as the basis for all other attainments. At the same time, spiritual endeavors such as contemplative prayer, inner personal transformation and *teshuvah* are important. This section includes detailed explanation of a very accessible approach to contemplation in prayer.

The remaining nine chapters of part two discuss the dif-

---

9. *Hayom Yom,* 15 *Adar II.* See also *On Learning Chassidus* (Kehot) pp.53-4.

ferent levels of Love and Fear of the Divine, and the power of *teshuvah*. This is explained by the second half of the opening verse: *G-d illuminates my darkness*. The climax is that not only is the darkness illuminated, but "the darkness itself shines." This theme is explained in light of the specific events of the story of Chanukah.

The image of the lamp, expounded successively in the *Zohar, Tanya, Torah Or* and here in *Shaarei Orah*, is a powerful theme. Together with the many other ideas presented in this *maamar*, here is an extended teaching which can help any person to evaluate and enhance his or her life as a Jew today.

NOTE ON THE HEBREW TEXT: In vowelizing the Hebrew words in this edition we have followed the grammatical rules of the Holy Tongue, which occasionally differ from the traditional or colloquial pronunciation. The original footnotes to the Hebrew text appear at the end of the maamar.

TRANSLATION AND COMMENTARY

INTRODUCTION TO CHAPTER ONE

R. DovBer begins with two questions on the verse, *For You, G-d, are my Lamp; and G-d will illuminate my darkness.* The first question is: Why is G-d's Name invoked twice, seemingly splitting the verse into two separate statements?

To answer, R. DovBer quotes the verse, *The soul of man is a Lamp of G-d.* He explains that the four letters of the Divine Name are manifested in the Jew. Each letter corresponds to a different aspect of the inner person. This is what is meant by, *For You, G-d, are my Lamp.* When a person sins, the letters can become defective but can be repaired through *teshuvah*. This is the meaning of the second half of the verse, *and G-d will illuminate my darkness,* i.e., when the person performs *teshuvah.*

R. DovBer then describes the lamp, saying that it consists of five parts: 1) the wick; 2) the flame, which consists of two parts: the dark radiance that burns close to the wick, consuming it, and 3) the flame's bright radiance; 4) the oil; 5) the vessel (that contains the oil and wick).

1.
THE CHANUKAH LAMP AND THE SOUL

QUESTIONS

"For You, G-d, are my lamp; and G-d will illuminate my darkness."[1] We can ask: Why is G-d's Name invoked twice? The verse ought to read: "For You, G-d are my lamp, Who will illuminate my darkness." Further, what is the meaning of the conjunctive "and" in the phrase "*and* G-d will illuminate"? Why not simply say, "G-d will illuminate"?

THE DIVINE NAME IN THE SOUL

Says King Solomon: "The lamp of G-d is the soul of a person."[2] The soul is literally termed "the lamp of G-d" because within it[3] the four letters of *Havaya* shine.[4] *Yud* is expressed by *chochmah*[5] in the brain; *hey* by *binah*[6]; *vav* is expressed by the emotions in the heart; and the second *hey* is expressed by the person's actions.[7] This is the *tzelem el-*

---

1. II Samuel 22:29.

2. Proverbs 20:27.

3. The four letters of *Havaya* constitute the soul. *Yud* is *chochmah* of the soul—the power of self-sacrifice in every Jew. *Hey* is *binah* of the soul—the comprehension of G-dly Wisdom. *Vav* is the emotional attributes, and the latter *hey* is thought, speech and action of the soul. (*Pokeach Ivrim*, excerpt from Rabbi Yosef Yitzchak's diary, footnote 8). See also footnote 7 below.

4. HAVAYA. The Ineffable Divine Name, or Tetragrammaton, composed of the four letters Y-H-V-H, and colloquially pronounced *Havaya*. There are many Hebrew names for G-d in Scripture, each of which expresses a different aspect or attribute of the Divinity. *Havaya* refers to G-d the Infinite, transcending creation and nature, time and space completely—the level of Divinity which brings everything into existence *ex nihilo*. The name *Elokim* represents the level of G-d which conceals the Infinite Light and life-force, for this Infinite force is too intense for finite creatures to endure. *Elokim* is the power of G-d that makes the world appear to exist naturally and independently. Therefore, *Elokim* has the numerical value of the word *hateva* (nature). In the Era of Moshiach, however, the level of *Havaya* will be revealed and perceived throughout nature.

5. CHOCHMAH: *Chochmah* in human terms refers to the highest level of the thinking process, the initial, unstructured flash of insight. In the process of creation it may be loosely defined as a seminal, highly condensed revelation of immanent G-dly light on its highest level that is the life force of all of creation.

6. BINAH. The second step in the thinking process and the development of the seminal thought of *chochmah*, also symbolizing *yesh*, the existential entity.

7. The Tetragrammaton is composed of four letters: The *yud*, a simple point, symbolizes His Wisdom, the state of concealment and obscurity, before it develops into a state of ex-

(א)

כְּתִיב כִּי אַתָּה נֵרִי הוי״ה וַה׳ יַגִּיהַּ חָשְׁכִּי הִנֵּה יֵשׁ לְהָבִין מַה שֶּׁכָּפַל הַדִּבּוּר לוֹמַר ב׳ פְּעָמִים הוי״ה כִּי אַתָּה נֵרִי הוי״ה וַה׳ יַגִּיהַּ כו׳ הֲוָה לֵיהּ לְמֵימַר כִּי אַתָּה נֵרִי ה׳ יַגִּיהַּ חָשְׁכִּי וְעוֹד מַהוּ הַוָּי״ו דְּוַה׳ יַגִּיהַּ בְּתוֹסֶפֶת וָי״ו הֲוָה לֵיהּ לְמֵימַר ה׳ יַגִּיהַּ כו׳.

וְהִנֵּה כְּתִיב כִּי נֵר ה׳ נִשְׁמַת אָדָם שֶׁנְּשָׁמָה שֶׁבְּאָדָם נִקְרָא נֵר הוי״ה מַמָּשׁ שֶׁמֵּאִיר בָּהּ ד׳ אוֹתִיּוֹת דְּשֵׁם הוי״ה יוּ״ד בְּחָכְמָה שֶׁבְּמוֹחַ וְהֵ״א בְּבִינָה וָי״ו בְּמִדּוֹת שֶׁבְּלֵב הֵ״א אַחֲרוֹנָה בְּמַעֲשֶׂה וְהוּא עִיקַּר בְּחִינַת צֶלֶם אֱלֹקִים שֶׁבְּאָדָם

---

pansion and revelation in comprehension.

When the "point" evolves into a state of expansion and revelation of comprehension in the concealed words, it is then contained and represented in the letter *hey*. The shape of the letter has dimension, expansion in breadth, which implies the breadth of explanation and understanding, and expansion in length, to indicate extension and flow downward into the concealed worlds.

In the next stage this extension and flow are drawn still lower into the revealed worlds. This may be compared to one who wishes to reveal his thoughts to another through his speech, for example. This stage of extension is contained and represented in the final letters *vav* and *hey*.

Vav, in shape a vertical line, indicates downward extension. Also, this downward flow is effected through the divine traits of benevolence and goodness and His other sacred traits, included in general terms in the verse, "Yours O G-d is the greatness…" until "Yours O G-d is the dominion…," until, but not inclusive. His seventh attribute, *malchut* or dominion, is called the "Word of G-d," as in the verse, "Wherever the word of the king holds sway."

This attribute of dominion is contained and represented in the final *hey* of the Tetragrammaton.

These same four stages apply to the soul of man, i.e., the divine soul that "He blew from within Himself." There is the initial state of hidden concept symbolized in the letter *yud*, with its potential of being revealed, thus understanding and conceiving of His true being and greatness, each person according to his measure, according to the breadth of his intellect and understanding.

As man deepens his intelligence, as he broadens his mind and comprehension, to contemplate His greatness, his now developed understanding is indicated in the letter *hey*, that has breadth. The *hey* also has length to indicate downward extension, that from his understanding and contemplation of G-d's majesty, he arouses love and fear and their ramifications in his mind and in the recesses of his heart.

In the following stage these emotions would actually become manifest in his heart.

okim,[8] the divine form within the person, symbolically constituting four letters. If one causes a flaw in his soul in the letter *yud*, such as by profaning the Shabbat or by not studying Torah,[9] the divine radiance of the *yud* is withdrawn. Or, if one causes a flaw in the letter *hey* [the divine radiance of that letter is withdrawn], and so on, as we say in the confession of the Shema prayer before retiring at night.[10]

Thus, "and G-d will illuminate my darkness"–even after the radiance of *tzelem elokim* in the four letters of *Havaya* has been flawed. For this reason the verse repeats itself, first stating, "You G-d are my lamp," and then [after the initial radiance is withdrawn, through transgression], as a result of *teshuvah*, "G-d will illuminate my darkness."[11]

THE SOUL AS A SHINING LIGHT

We have to understand how the four letters of *Havaya* are vested in the soul. First,[12] let us consider the nature of the souls of the Jewish people, which corresponded to the seven lights of the Menorah in the Temple. What indeed is the true nature of these lamps? As the Sages comment: "Does He need light?"[13] Rather, the Menorah is actually a testimony to the Jewish people that the *Shechinah*[14] dwells among them.[15]

FOUR ASPECTS OF THE LAMP

At this point we should understand that in a lamp there are, in gen-

---

This leads to the true service of G-d, in Torah study and mitzvah observance, with voice and speech, or with deed. This is the import of the letters *vav hey*. (*Iggeret HaTeshuvah*, ch. 4)

8. Lit., "in the image of G-d"—see Genesis 1:27.

9. *Bittul Torah* in Hebrew. See *Tanya* chapter 8.

10. See *Mishnat Chasidim, Masechet Hash'chivah* chapter 6; *Shaar Hakavanot, Inyan Derushei Leilah* section 5, (also in *Tehilat Hashem* p. 140) where the individual repents for transgressions which cause flaws in the four letters of the Divine Name: neglect of *Keriat Shema* (*yud*); neglect of *tefillin* (*hey*); neglect of *tzitzit* (*vav*); neglect of Prayer (*hey*). This reflects Igeret *HaTeshuvah*, ch. 7, 98a: "For this reason the order of *Kriat Shema* at the bedside includes acceptance of the four executions of the Court... Besides, according to mystical interpretation, impairing the *yud* of the Name (Tetragrammaton) is like incurring lapidation; impairing the *hey* is like incurring burning; impairing the *vav* is like incurring the sword, and the latter *hey*, is like incurring strangulation. Neglecting the Shema impairs the *yud*, and the *tefillin* the *hey*, *tzitzit* the *vav*, and worship the latter *hey*...." However, see *Likkutei Torah, Derushim L'Shabbat Shuvah*, 64d which includes neglect of Torah study among the transgressions affecting the

וְאִם פָּגַם בְּנַפְשׁוֹ בְּיוּ"ד כְּמוֹ בְּחִילּוּל שַׁבָּת אוֹ בְּבִיטּוּל תַּלְמוּד תּוֹרָה נִסְתַּלֵּק אוֹר הָאֱלֹקִי שֶׁבִּי' אוֹ שֶׁפָּגַם בְּהֵ"א כו' וּכְמוֹ שֶׁאוֹמְרִים בְּוִידּוּי בִּקְרִיאַת שְׁמַע שֶׁעַל הַמִּטָּה כַּיָּדוּעַ.

וְזֶהוּ וַה' יַגִּיהַּ חָשְׁכִּי גַּם לְאַחַר שֶׁנִּפְגַּם הָאוֹר דְּצֶלֶם אֱלֹקִים שֶׁבְּד' אוֹתִיּוֹת דְּשֵׁם הוי"ה וְעַל כֵּן כָּפַל הַדִּבּוּר וְאָמַר כִּי אַתָּה נֵרִי הוי"ה וַה' יַגִּיהַּ חָשְׁכִּי עַל יְדֵי תְּשׁוּבָה וְדַי לַמֵּבִין.

וְהִנֵּה בֶּאֱמֶת יֵשׁ לְהָבִין אֵיךְ מְלוּבָּשִׁים ד' אוֹתִיּוֹת דְּשֵׁם הוי"ה בְּנִשְׁמַת אָדָם וְיֵשׁ לְהַקְדִּים תְּחִלָּה בְּשֹׁרֶשׁ כְּלָלוּת עִנְיַן נִשְׁמוֹת יִשְׂרָאֵל שֶׁהֵן ז' נֵרוֹת הַמְּנוֹרָה שֶׁבַּמִּקְדָּשׁ כַּיָּדוּעַ וְיֵשׁ לְהָבִין תְּחִלָּה שֹׁרֶשׁ עִנְיַן הַנֵּרוֹת דִּמְנוֹרָה שֶׁאָמְרוּ רַבּוֹתֵינוּ זִכְרוֹנָם לִבְרָכָה וְכִי לְאוֹרָהּ הוּא צָרִיךְ אֶלָּא עֵדוּת הִיא לְיִשְׂרָאֵל שֶׁהַשְּׁכִינָה שׁוֹרָה בָּהֶם כו'.

וְיֵשׁ לְהַקְדִּים תְּחִלָּה שֶׁיֵּשׁ בְּאוֹר הַנֵּר בִּכְלָל ד' דְּבָרִים הָא' הַפְּתִילָה הַדּוֹלֶקֶת עַל יְדֵי הָאוֹר שֶׁנֶּאֱחָז וְנִדְלָק בָּהּ וְהַב' הָאוֹר עַצְמוֹ הַדּוֹלֵק בַּפְּתִילָה וְיֵשׁ ב' מַדְרֵיגוֹת בָּאוֹר הַזֶּה וְהֵן ב' מִינֵי גַּוְונֵי אוֹר א' גַּוָּון הַשָּׁחוֹר שֶׁסָּמוּךְ לַפְּתִילָה

---

letter *yud*, for "Torah is derived from *chochmah*"—the *yud* (*Zohar* II:85a, 121a). See also *Likkutei Torah*, *Derushim L'Rosh Hashana* 59a.

11. This briefly answers the first question. The general theme of this verse is expounded through the following chapters. The second question—why the second half of the verse includes a *vav*, '*and* G-d'—is answered in chapter 18 of this *maamar*.

12. The author now proceeds to explain the nature of an oil lamp, comprised of a wick, oil, a flame and a vessel, by which we will be able to comprehend the relationship of *Havaya* to the soul.

13. *Shabbat* 22b.

14. SHECHINAH, Divine Presence, is the immanent category of the Divine influence, brought down to earth by the study of the Torah and the practice of *mitzvot*. In addition to *Shechinah* being identified with *malchut* and the source of the souls, *Shechinah* corresponds to the second letter *hay* of the Tetragrammaton, Y-H-V-H. The sinner, on the other hand, breaks up the unity of the Divine Name, dragging down the *Shechinah* into "exile."

15. *Shabbat* ibid.: "a testimony to the inhabitants of the world that the *Shechinah* dwells among the Jewish people." Cf. *Kiddushin* 70b, and *Likkutei Torah*, *Pekudei* 4b.

eral, four aspects. The first is the wick, which illuminates because of the flame that burns from it. Then there is the flame itself that burns from the wick, which includes two levels, expressed in two colors of the light.[16] One is the dark color which is close to the wick, and is called "dark radiance," which burns and gradually consumes the wick; the other, higher up, is the white flame, which is called "the light which illuminates" and also the "bright radiance." The fourth aspect of the lamp is the oil which flows into the wick and is absorbed in it. Without the oil, the flame would not burn from the wick at all, but would leap away[17] and be extinguished.

Through bonding and connecting these four aspects—i.e.: the oil, the wick, and two colors of flame—there is manifest "light." For if the flame did not cleave to the wick there would be no light at all—it would vanish altogether. Only when the flame cleaves to the wick, consuming it gradually, can this flame be termed "illuminating light" which is the essential quality of light. This quality is achieved particularly by the lower aspect of the flame, the "dark radiance" which holds to the wick and burns from it, gradually consuming it.

OIL

However, it is the oil which achieves the bonding of the two-tiered flame with the wick. Without oil the flame would either vanish, or swiftly consume the wick, extinguishing the light. But when the oil flows through the wick, the flame is drawn towards it and burns properly. The wick does not quickly burn away, and the flame lasts a long time.

This is a paradoxical process: the oil draws the flame to cleave well to the wick,[18] and on the other hand prevents the wick from being swiftly burned up.[19] A further effect of the oil is that by drawing from it, the flame becomes it particularly bright and pure. This is the white flame which shines due to the purity of the oil. The oil thus has two different effects: one is causing the [dark] flame to cleave to the wick [i.e. preventing it from consuming the wick and thus] ex-

16. See *Zohar* I:51a.

17. The flame originates in the sphere of fire beyond the world. In order to shine in our plane of existence it has to be "caught" by the wick. Yet its natural tendency is always to

שֶׁנִּקְרָא נְהוֹרָא אוּכָמָא הַשּׂוֹרֵף וּמְכַלֶּה לַפְּתִילָה מְעַט מְעַט וְהַב' אוֹר הַלָּבָן שֶׁלְּמַעְלָה שֶׁנִּקְרָא אוֹר הַמֵּאִיר וְנִקְרָא נְהוֹרָא חִוְּורָא וְהַד' הוּא הַשֶּׁמֶן שֶׁנִּמְשָׁךְ אַחַר הַפְּתִילָה וְנִבְלָע בָּהּ שֶׁאִם לֹא הַשֶּׁמֶן לֹא הָיָה הָאוֹר דּוֹלֵק בַּפְּתִילָה כְּלָל אֶלָּא הָיָה קוֹפֵץ וּמִסְתַּלֵּק כַּיָּדוּעַ.

וְהִנֵּה בְּאֶמְצָעוּת חִיבּוּר וְקֶשֶׁר ד' דְּבָרִים אֵלּוּ הַיְינוּ שֶׁמֶן וּפְתִילָה וּב' גְּוָונֵי אוֹר הַנַּ"ל הוּא הַנִּקְרָא בְּשֵׁם אוֹר בִּכְלָל כִּי אִם לֹא הָיָה הָאוֹר נֶאֱחָז בַּפְּתִילָה לֹא נִקְרָא אוֹר כְּלָל מִצַּד עַצְמוֹ כִּי הוּא קוֹפֵץ לְגַמְרֵי רַק כַּאֲשֶׁר הָאוֹר נֶאֱחָז בַּפְּתִילָה וְדוֹלֵק אֶת הַפְּתִילָה לְכַלּוֹתָהּ מְעַט מְעַט כַּנַּ"ל אֲזַי עַל יְדֵי הַדְלָקָה זוֹ שֶׁדָּלַק בָּהּ הָאוֹר נִקְרָא בְּשֵׁם אוֹר הַמֵּאִיר שֶׁזֶּהוּ עִיקַּר שֵׁם אוֹר וְהוּא בָּא דַּוְקָא עַל יְדֵי אוֹר הַתַּחְתּוֹן שֶׁנִּקְרָא נְהוֹרָא אוּכָמָא שֶׁנֶּאֱחָז בַּפְּתִילָה וְדוֹלֵק בָּהּ בְּכִלָּיוֹן מְעַט מְעַט כו'.

אַךְ סִיבַּת הַקֶּשֶׁר וְחִיבּוּר הָאוֹר בַּפְּתִילָה בְּב' גְּוָונִין הַנַּ"ל הוּא רַק עַל יְדֵי הַשֶּׁמֶן דַּוְקָא שֶׁבְּלֹא שֶׁמֶן הָיָה הָאוֹר קוֹפֵץ לְגַמְרֵי מִיָּד אוֹ שֶׁהָיָה שׂוֹרֵף וּמְכַלֶּה לְהַפְּתִילָה לְגַמְרֵי כְּרֶגַע וּמִסְתַּלֵּק אַךְ עַל יְדֵי הַשֶּׁמֶן שֶׁהוּא נִשְׁאָב בַּפְּתִילָה הוּא סִיבַּת אֲחִיזַת הָאוֹר הֵיטֵב בַּפְּתִילָה לְהַדְלִיקָהּ וְאֵינוֹ קוֹפֵץ כְּלָל מִפְּנֵי שֶׁהָאוֹר נִמְשָׁךְ אַחַר הַשֶּׁמֶן לִשְׁאוֹב אוֹתוֹ וּלְכַלּוֹתוֹ מְעַט מְעַט וְעַל יְדֵי זֶה אֵין הַפְּתִילָה כָּלָה מְהֵרָה וְנִמְשָׁךְ זְמַן הַהַדְלָקָה.

וְיֵשׁ בָּזֶה דָּבָר וְהִיפּוּכוֹ שֶׁהַשֶּׁמֶן מַמְשִׁיךְ הָאוֹר לִהְיוֹת נֶאֱחָז הֵיטֵב בַּפְּתִילָה וְגַם מַה שֶּׁיְּכַלֶּה וְיִשְׂרוֹף לַפְּתִילָה וְלִשְׁאוֹב הַשֶּׁמֶן כו' וְעוֹד תּוֹעֶלֶת שֵׁנִי בַּשֶּׁמֶן שֶׁעַל יְדֵי שְׁאִיבַת הָאוֹר אוֹתוֹ נַעֲשֶׂה בּוֹ אוֹר בָּהִיר וְזַךְ בְּיוֹתֵר וְהוּא אוֹר הַלָּבָן הַמֵּאִיר שֶׁהוּא בָּא לְפִי עֵרֶךְ צְלִילַת הַשֶּׁמֶן דַּוְקָא כַּיָּדוּעַ וְנִמְצָא עַל יְדֵי הַשֶּׁמֶן יֵשׁ ב' מִינֵי תּוֹעֶלֶת א' סִיבַּת חִיבּוּר

move away from the wick back towards its source. See *Tanya* ch. 19.

18. I.e., to behave contrary to its nature.

19. I.e., in order to create a "lamp," not a fire.

tending the time that the flame will burn; and the other is generating the bright pure radiance, which illuminates.

(A burning piece of wood is just a burning fire, which is not considered to be giving as much illumination as the light of a lamp of oil and wick. This is the difference between light and fire.)

So it is understood that the oil joins the two-colored radiance with the wick: a) it connects the black fire of the flame to the wick, which burns and consumes the wick as long as it is joined to it, and is also the main contact of the flame with the wick; b) it connects the higher bright radiance to the wick, and is also the source of its brightness.

This double effect comes from the consumption of the oil in the flame. The oil is drawn through the wick, attracted by the flame, which produces the two colors of light described above. In fact, these two kinds of flame are both initially included in the oil. The effect of burning the oil is that the two kinds of flame emerge from concealment and are now revealed.

CHANUKAH

On account of this quality of the oil, the Sages decreed concerning the mitzvah of the Chanukah lamp that there are some oils which one may not use, because they do not flow properly in a wick.[20] In the Chanukah lamp it is important that there should be the two colors of flame around the wick, and that the light should last a certain time. This is impossible without good, clear oil which flows in the wick, as will be explained.[21]

A FIFTH ASPECT

(There is also a fifth aspect of the [Chanukah] lamp—and this is the vessel of the lamp itself, containing within it all the other four aspects: the oil, the wick, and the two kinds of flame. Without the vessel of the lamp there would be no light at all.[22])

---

20. *Shabbat* 21a. See *Maamarei Admur Ha'emtza'ee*, *Bereishit* p. 362.

21. In chapter 3 the oil will be explained in spiritual terms, as *chochmah* of the soul, con-

וְקֶשֶׁר הָאוֹר בַּפְּתִילָה וְהַמְשָׁכַת זְמַן דְּלִיקָתוֹ כַּנַּ"ל וְהַב' מַה שֶּׁיֵּשׁ בָּאוֹר אוֹר הַלָּבָן הַזַּךְ הַנִּקְרָא אוֹר הַמֵּאִיר כַּנַּ"ל

(כִּי בְּעֵץ הַשּׂוֹרֵף וְדוֹלֵק אֵין בּוֹ רַק אֵשׁ הַשּׂוֹרֵף וְלֹא נִקְרָא אוֹר הַמֵּאִיר כָּל כַּךְ כְּאוֹר הַנֵּר בְּשֶׁמֶן וּפְתִילָה וְהוּא הַהֶפְרֵשׁ בֵּין אֵשׁ לְאוֹר)

וַהֲרֵי מוּבָן עַל כָּל פָּנִים שֶׁעַל יְדֵי הַשֶּׁמֶן מִתְחַבֵּר הָאוֹר בַּפְּתִילָה בְּב' גְּוָונֵי אוֹר הַנַּ"ל א' חִיבּוּר אֵשׁ הַשָּׁחוֹר שֶׁבָּאוֹר הַשּׂוֹרֵף שֶׁיּוּמְשַׁךְ זְמַן אֲחִיזָתוֹ לְכַלּוֹת הַפְּתִילָה כַּנַּ"ל שֶׁזֶּהוּ עִיקַּר חִיבּוּר הָאוֹר בַּפְּתִילָה וְהַב' חִיבּוּר אוֹר הָעֶלְיוֹן הַלָּבָן וְסִיבַּת בְּהִירָתוֹ כַּנַּ"ל.

שֶׁזֶּהוּ בָּא מִצַּד כִּלְיוֹן הַשֶּׁמֶן בָּאוֹר כַּאֲשֶׁר נִשְׁאָב בַּפְּתִילָה וְהָאוֹר מוֹשֵׁךְ אוֹתוֹ נַעֲשֶׂה בְּאוֹר זֶה ב' גְּוָונִין א' גַּוָּן הַשָּׁחוֹר שֶׁשּׁוֹאֵב וּמְכַלֶּה הַפְּתִילָה עִם הַשֶּׁמֶן הַמּוּבְלָע בָּהּ וְהַב' גַּוָּן הָאוֹר הָעֶלְיוֹן שֶׁהוּא בָּהִיר וְזַךְ כְּפִי צְלִילַת הַשֶּׁמֶן כַּנַּ"ל וְאִם כֵּן הֲרֵי וַדַּאי כָּלוּל הָיָה בַּשֶּׁמֶן תְּחִלָּה ב' גְּוָונֵי אוֹר הַלָּלוּ רַק שֶׁיָּצְאוּ מִן הַהֶעְלֵם לְגִילּוּי בָּאוֹר הַזֶּה עַל יְדֵי כִּלְיוֹן הַשֶּׁמֶן בָּאוֹר הַדּוֹלֵק כַּאֲשֶׁר נִשְׁאָב וְנִמְשָׁךְ אַחַר הַפְּתִילָה.

שֶׁבָּזֶה הַטַּעַם גָּזְרוּ אוֹמֶר בְּמִצְוַת נֵר חֲנוּכָּה שֶׁיֵּשׁ שְׁמָנִים שֶׁאֵין מַדְלִיקִים בָּהֶם לְפִי שֶׁאֵינָן נִמְשָׁכִים הֵיטֵב אַחַר הַפְּתִילָה לְפִי שֶׁבְּנֵר חֲנוּכָּה צָרִיךְ לִהְיוֹת ב' גְּוָונֵי אוֹר בַּפְּתִילָה וְשֶׁיּוּמְשַׁךְ זְמַן הַדְלָקָתוֹ שֶׁאִי אֶפְשָׁר בְּלֹא שֶׁמֶן טוֹב וְצָלוּל שֶׁנִּמְשָׁךְ אַחַר הַפְּתִילָה מִטַּעַם שֶׁיִּתְבָּאֵר בְּעֶזְרַת ה' וְדַי לַמֵּבִין.

(וְיֵשׁ עוֹד דָּבָר חֲמִישִׁי וְהוּא כְּלִי הַנֵּר עַצְמוֹ שֶׁהוּא הַמַּחֲזִיק בְּתוֹכוֹ כָּל ד' דְּבָרִים הַנַּ"ל הַשֶּׁמֶן וְהַפְּתִילָה וְאוֹר הַכָּלוּל מִב' גַּוָּונִין הַנַּ"ל שֶׁבִּלְעָדוֹ לֹא יִתְקַיֵּים הָאוֹר כְּלָל):

taining two different kinds of spiritual radiance.

22. The theme of the vessel of the lamp is expanded at the end of chapter 6 below.

SUMMARY
OF CHAPTER ONE

For You, G-d, are my lamp; and G-d will illuminate my darkness.

Question: Why is the verse bisected? Why invoke G-d's name twice? And what is the implication of the conjunctive '*and*'?

Answer: Man is created in the Divine form. The soul contains the four letters of the Divine Name *Havaya*. *Yud*—wisdom; *hey*—comprehension; *vav*—emotions; *hey*—action.

If a soul becomes flawed and darkened by sin, it can be repaired through *teshuvah*. This is implied by "*and G-d will illuminate my darkness.*"

The soul of man is a lamp of G-d. The Rebbe analyzes the lamp structure to help us understand the soul.

An oil lamp has five parts:

1) the vessel (holding oil and wick);

2) the wick;

3) the dark radiance, burning close to the wick and consuming it;

4) the illuminating radiance;

5) the oil.

The oil has two functions:

1) The oil plays a conflicting role, as it both fuels the destruction of the wick and yet ultimately sustains it. The oil causes the flame to act against its nature, i.e., to remain attached to the wick; and it sustains the wick, enabling it to be consumed only gradually.

2) The quality of the flame depends on the quality of the oil. Thus, the oil itself must possess multiple colors or qualities that eventually appear in the burning flame.

INTRODUCTION TO CHAPTER TWO

R. DovBer now begins to explain the image of the physical lamp in terms of the spiritual life of the person. This description will continue through the entire discourse.

The two aspects of the flame represent two aspects of the spirituality of the soul: the bright radiance is the Divine Soul expressing its most sublime sacred attainment, as in its total surrender to the Divine when saying *Echad* (One) in the Shema, while the dark radiance, which consumes the wick, expresses the enthusiasm of the Divine Soul as it is vested in the Animal Soul. Here there is a sense of struggle and the transformation of negative emotions. This is expressed by the way the dark flame interacts with and eats away at the wick.

Both flames require oil, the theme of Chapter Three.

2.
TWO FLAMES OF THE SOUL

The physical configuration of the lamp can be understood regarding both the Divine radiance within the individual soul of man—called the actual "lamp of G-d"—and the Divine radiance, within the supernal source of all souls, *malchut*[23] of *Atzilut*[24].

For it is known that every Divine soul[25] has a source in the Living G-d, the source of life of all the souls, as expressed in the words "You created [the Soul], You formed it... You breathed it into me,"[26] and, as it is written "Light is sown for the righteous (*tzaddik*),"[27] meaning [both] the supernal *tzaddik* and the lower *tzaddik*,[28] as it is written "Your people are all *tzaddikim*."[29]

These are the two colors of light discussed above: one, the "white radiance," which is truly Divine radiance, as it is written "You [G-d] illuminate my lamp"[30] or "For You, G-d, are my lamp."[31] This is the Divine ecstasy,[32] which is essentially present in the "spark" of every single Jewish soul—even the most lowly—totally beyond reason and understanding. On account of this power one can surrender his soul [when saying] "One" [in the Shema] with great, delightful love[33] with all his soul, exercising total *teshuvah* from the innards of his heart until he [almost] faints.[34]

---

23. MALCHUT. Literally, Royalty or Kingship; the tenth and last of the ten sefirot. *Malchut* is referred to in the *Tikkunei Zohar* (intro. 17a) as the "Mouth of G-d," the Word or speech of G-d by which the world comes into actual being. (Mouth and speech are used for communication with "others" outside of the self.) The world and the creatures (the "others") make it possible to speak of a Divine Kingdom; since "there cannot be a King without a nation," G-d cannot be a ruler without the element of "other."

24. *Malchut* of *Atzilut*, the source of Jewish souls, also known as *Knesset Yisrael*, the "community of Israel" in a spiritual sense, the source from which individual souls descend and are sustained, sometimes identified with the *Shechinah* (Divine Presence) itself. See also footnote 14. *Malchut*, the source of Jewish souls, is also called *matronita*, queen, for "all of Israel are princes" (*Mishna*, *Shabbat* 14:4).

25. Every Jew has two souls, an "animal soul" which is clothed in the blood of a human being, giving life to the body, and a divine, or "G-dly soul," which is a part of G-d above, as it is written, "And He breathed into his nostrils the breath of life." See *Tanya*, chapters 1-2 at length.

26. Liturgy, Morning Blesings. I.e., since G-d created it, its source is G-d.

(ב)

וְהִנֵּה הַנִּמְשָׁל מִכָּל הַנַּ"ל בְּאוֹר הַנֵּר הַגַּשְׁמִי יוּבַן הַכֹּל בְּאוֹר הָאֱלֹקִי שֶׁבְּנִשְׁמַת אָדָם בִּפְרָט שֶׁנִּקְרָא נֵר הוי"ה מַמָּשׁ (וּבִכְלָל בִּמְקוֹר נִשְׁמוֹת יִשְׂרָאֵל לְמַעְלָה שֶׁהוּא בְּחִינַת מַלְכוּת דַּאֲצִילוּת).

דְּהִנֵּה יָדוּעַ שֶׁכָּל נְשָׁמָה הָאֱלֹקִית יֵשׁ לָהּ שֹׁרֶשׁ וּמָקוֹר בֵּאלֹקִים חַיִּים מְקוֹר כָּל חַיֵּי הַנְּשָׁמוֹת כְּמוֹ אַתָּה בְרָאתָ יְצַרְתָּ כו' נְפַחְתָּ בִּי כו' וּכְמוֹ שֶׁכָּתוּב אוֹר זָרוּעַ לַצַּדִּיק כו' צַדִּיק עֶלְיוֹן וְצַדִּיק תַּחְתּוֹן וְזֶהוּ שֶׁנֶּאֱמַר וְעַמֵּךְ כּוּלָּם צַדִּיקִים.

וְהֵן ב' גַּוְונֵי אוֹר הַנַּ"ל א' נְהוֹרָא חִוְּורָא שֶׁהוּא אוֹר הָאֱלֹקִי מַמָּשׁ וּכְמוֹ שֶׁכָּתוּב כִּי אַתָּה תָּאִיר נֵרִי אוֹ כִּי אַתָּה נֵרִי ה' כו' וְהַיְינוּ בְּחִינַת הִתְפַּעֲלוּת אֱלֹקוּת שֶׁיֵּשׁ בְּעֶצֶם בְּכָל נִיצוֹץ קָטָן שֶׁבְּיִשְׂרָאֵל לְמַעְלָה מִן הַטַּעַם וָדַעַת כְּלָל שֶׁמֵּחֲמַת זֶה הַכֹּחַ יוּכַל לִמְסוֹר נַפְשׁוֹ בְּאֶחָד בְּאַהֲבָה רַבָּה בְּתַעֲנוּגִים בְּכָל נַפְשׁוֹ כו' וְלָשׁוּב בִּתְשׁוּבָה שְׁלֵימָה מִקִּירַת

---

27. Psalms 97:11. See Zohar III:197a.

28. *Tzaddik elyon* and *tzaddik tachton* in the Hebrew. *Tzaddik elyon* is the term given to a soul before its descent into a body, whereas *tzaddik tachton* is the term given to a soul vested in a body. (*Maamarei Admur Hazaken Al Parshiyot HaTorah*, vol. 2, p. 895)

29. Isaiah 60:21. The term "*tzaddik*" refers to every Jew, as above, and the fact that "light is sown for every Jew" implies that the soul of every Jew is rooted in the Living G-d.

30. Psalms 18:29.

31. II Samuel 22:29

32. HITPA'ALUT: Any form of "being moved." The term includes enthusiasm, excitement and spiritual ecstasy.

33. AHAVA B'TAANUGIM: In *Tanya*, chapter 9, Rabbi Schneur Zalman distinguishes various degrees of love: *ahava azah*—ardent love; *ahava rabbah*—great love, also called *ahava b'taanugim*—delightful love, a serene love of fulfillment. The first is likened to a burning flame, while the second is likened to calm waters.

34. KELOT HANEFESH: Lit., "expiring of the soul." This term is used for an intense otherworldly passion. See *Tanya* chapter 3: "when the intellect deeply contemplates and immerses itself exceedingly in the greatness of

This [flame] is called the "illuminating radiance" which depends on the purity of the oil.

TRANSFORMING THE HEART

The second kind of flame is the "dark radiance" which burns and consumes. This corresponds to the vesting of the Divine soul in the vital and natural soul, which stems from *Kelipat Nogah*.[35] This is the ecstasy which results from grasping a Divine idea with human intellect in the physical brain and the emotions of the heart of flesh. [The heart has a] natural heat, "for the inclination of man's heart is evil from his youth"[36]—it is drawn after any evil desire.[37]

Sometimes, when the power of the bad feelings becomes dominant, in material desires—without any arousal of *teshuvah*[38]—then the Divine radiance in the soul can be completely and utterly darkened (as it is written "the lamp of the wicked is extinguished"[39]; the flame goes out completely). On the other hand, sometimes the power of Divine radiance in the Divine soul becomes dominant over the natural soul, and this causes an excitement of fiery flames of longing for G-d alone, until one comes to despise evil.[40] His heart is quelled so that it will not be drawn at all after any foreign desire.

[In this state] both his mind and his natural, material feelings are excited with a Divine ecstasy, and are absorbed [in goodness] and transformed from evil to good, changing their negative nature from one extreme to another. This is because of the radiance [of the soul] that burns and consumes, like the example of the black fire which

---

G-d, how he fills all the worlds, and in the presence of Whom everything is considered nothing—there will be born and aroused in his mind and thought the emotion of awe for the Divine Majesty, to fear and be humble before His blessed greatness, which is without end or limit, and to have the dread of G-d in his heart. Next, his heart will glow with an intense love, like burning coals, with a passion, desire and longing, and a yearning soul, towards the greatness of *Ein Sof* blessed be He. This constitutes the culminating passion of the soul, of which Scripture speaks, as 'My soul longs and faints...' and 'My soul thirsts for G-d...' and 'My soul thirsts for you...' This thirst is derived from the element of fire, which is found in the Divine soul."

When one recites the Shema, which is of this theme, and truly contemplates its meaning, i.e., the aforementioned, it can cause *kelot hanefesh*.

35. KELIPAT NOGAH AND THE THREE IMPURE KELIPOT. *Kelipah*, or "shell" is the symbol frequently used in Kabbalah to denote "evil" and the source of sensual desires in human nature. *Kelipat Nogah*, "translucent shell," contains some good and, unlike the Three Impure *Kelipot*, which are entirely evil, is "neutral" and can be utilized for holiness.

Everything in one realm has a cor-

לִבּוֹ עַד כַּלּוֹתוֹ וכו׳ וְהוּא נִקְרָא אוֹר הַמֵּאִיר שֶׁזֶּה תָּלוּי לְפִי עֶרֶךְ צְלִילַת הַשֶּׁמֶן כַּנַּ״ל.

הַבּ׳ אֵשׁ שָׁחוֹר הַנַּ״ל שֶׁהוּא הַשּׂוֹרֵף וּמְכַלֶּה כו׳ וְהַיְינוּ עִנְיַן הִתְלַבְּשׁוּת הַנְּשָׁמָה הָאֱלֹקִית בַּנֶּפֶשׁ הַחִיּוּנִית הַטִּבְעִיּוּת שֶׁשָּׁרְשָׁהּ בִּקְלִיפַּת נוֹגַהּ בְּתַעֲרוּבוֹת טוֹב וָרָע כַּיָּדוּעַ וְהוּא הִתְפַּעֲלוּת הַשָּׂגָה אֱלֹקִית הַבָּא בַּשֵּׂכֶל הָאֱנוֹשִׁי שֶׁבְּמוֹחַ הַגַּשְׁמִי וּמִדּוֹת שֶׁבְּלֵב בָּשָׂר בַּחוֹם הַטִּבְעִי שֶׁיֵּצֶר לֵב הָאָדָם רַע מִנְּעוּרָיו לְהִתְמַשֵּׁךְ אַחַר כָּל תַּאֲוָה רָעָה כו׳.

וְלִפְרָקִים כַּאֲשֶׁר יִגְבַּר כֹּחַ הַמִּדּוֹת הָרָעוֹת בְּתַאֲוַת חוּמְרִיּוּת בְּלִי הִתְעוֹרְרוּת תְּשׁוּבָה לְגַמְרֵי יַחְשִׁיךְ לָאוֹר הָאֱלֹקִי שֶׁבַּנְּשָׁמָה לְגַמְרֵי מִכֹּל וָכֹל (וּכְמוֹ שֶׁכָּתוּב וְנֵר רְשָׁעִים יִדְעָךְ שֶׁקּוֹפֵץ לְגַמְרֵי כַּנַּ״ל) וּלְהֵיפֶךְ לִפְרָקִים כַּאֲשֶׁר יִגְבַּר כֹּחַ אוֹר הָאֱלֹקִי בַּנֶּפֶשׁ הָאֱלֹקִית עַל נֶפֶשׁ הַטִּבְעִית וְהוּא הִתְפַּעֲלוּת רִשְׁפֵּי אֵשׁ הַתְּשׁוּקָה לַה׳ לְבַדּוֹ עַד שֶׁמּוֹאֵס בָּרָע וְלָכוֹף לִבּוֹ שֶׁלֹּא יִמָּשֵׁךְ אַחַר כָּל רָצוֹן זָר כְּלָל וּכְלָל.

וְנִמְצָא שֶׁגַּם הַשֵּׂכֶל וּמִדּוֹת הַטִּבְעִיִּים הַחוּמְרִיִּים גַּם הֵם מִתְפַּעֲלִים בְּהִתְפַּעֲלוּת אֱלֹקוּת וְנִכְלָלִים וְנֶהְפָּכִים מֵרָע לְטוֹב לְשַׁנּוֹת טִבְעָם הָרָע מִן הַקָּצֶה לַקָּצֶה וְהַיְינוּ עַל יְדֵי בְּחִינַת אוֹר הַשּׂוֹרֵף וּמְכַלֶּה כְּמוֹ דִּמְיוֹן אֵשׁ הַשָּׁחוֹר הַשּׂוֹרֵף לַפְּתִילָה

---

responding opposite in another realm. The realm of holiness, sanctity, and purity is thus opposed by a realm of impurity. The realm of impurity itself is subdivided into two principal classes: the three altogether impure *Kelipot*, containing no good whatsoever in themselves, and *Kelipat Nogah*, an intermediate category between the three *Kelipot* mentioned and the order of holiness. Depending on the motives and actions of man, *Kelipat Nogah* is absorbed in one or the other of these two realms. It is a sort of potential *Kelipah*, which can be sublimated and developed for holiness, or may fall among the wholly impure *Kelipot*.

Man's animal soul stems from *Kelipat Nogah*. The Three *Kelipot*, however, can only be elevated by man's total rejection of them. See *Tanya* ch. 7.

36. Genesis 8:21.

37. The heart, i.e., the natural soul, contains a natural desire for evil. But when inspired by the Divine soul, the natural soul is consumed, similar to the dark fire that consumes the wick.

38. Which would help keep one's evil desires in check.

39. Proverbs 13:9.

40. One has attained a state of mind and feeling in which evil is no longer attractive, but rather loathsome.

burns the wick. This is called "the flame of G-d,"[41] which is aroused in the soul as an effect of comprehending the G-dly concept with a fiery ecstasy of Divine yearning. This flame, termed specifically "the flame of Y-H,"[42] burns and gradually consumes the fire and natural, evil foreign heat of the fleshly heart.

THE NEED FOR OIL

It is evident that anyone who becomes Divinely inspired, sensing a cleaving to G-d,[43] is moved even in his natural heart and mind with the very same excitement in a wave of true enthusiasm[44]—it just does not last very long.[45] Sometimes the radiance leaves after just a moment, and sometimes it remains a little longer. This brevity is because of a lack of "oil,"[46] for the body is compared to the wick, and the flame is the Divine radiance of the soul. [Joining the flame to the wick] is a mode of combining form[47] and matter.[48]

---

41. Song of Songs 8:6. The name of G-d used here is "Y-H," the first two letters of the Tetragrammaton.

42. In chapter 15, the *maamar* explains that the "flame of Y-H" is from *binah*, (the *yud* of the Divine Name representing *chochmah*, and the first *hey* representing *binah*). The power of *binah*, through the intensity and excitement of comprehension, is precisely to engender flames of enthusiasm which can transform one's inner feelings. This is generally achieved during *hitbonenut*, contemplation, which is from the same verbal root as *binah*.

43. *Devekut* in the Hebrew, a conscious sense of cleaving to the Divine during prayer, Torah study or observance of *mitzvot*. This is one of the central themes of early Chasidism. See also footnote 150.

44. R. DovBer was very concerned about distinguishing between "true" and "false" enthusiasm. See his Tract on Ecstasy (*Kuntres HaHitpa'alut, Maamarei Admur Ha'emtza'ee*, p. 39), which describes different levels of ecstasy or enthusiasm in prayer.

45. The reason why he is "also moved in his

הַנַּ"ל וְהוּא הַנִּקְרָא שַׁלְהֶבֶת יָ־הּ שֶׁבָּאָה בַּנְּשָׁמָה מִצַּד הַהַשָּׂגָה אֱלֹקִית בְּהִתְפַּעֲלוּת רִשְׁפֵּי אֵשׁ הַתְּשׁוּקָה אֱלֹקִית שַׁלְהֶבֶת זוֹ הַנִּקְרָא שַׁלְהֶבֶת יָ־הּ דַּוְקָא הוּא הַשּׂוֹרֵף וּמְכַלֶּה לָאֵשׁ וְחוּם זָר הָרָע הַטִּבְעִי שֶׁבְּלֵב בָּשָׂר מְעַט מְעַט כו׳.

וּכְמוֹ שֶׁאָנוּ רוֹאִים בְּחוּשׁ שֶׁכָּל מִי שֶׁמִּתְפָּעֵל בְּהִתְלַהֲבוּת וּדְבֵיקוּת הָאֱלֹקִי מִיָּד הוּא מִתְפָּעֵל בְּלִבּוֹ וּמוֹחוֹ הַטִּבְעִיִּים בְּהִתְלַהֲבוּת זוֹ מַמָּשׁ בְּהִתְפַּעֲלוּת אֲמִתִּית רַק שֶׁאֵינוֹ נִמְשָׁךְ זְמַן רַב רַק יֵשׁ כִּמְעַט רֶגַע קוֹפֵץ הָאוֹר וְיֵשׁ שֶׁמִּתְעַכֵּב מְעַט זְמַן יוֹתֵר וְזֶהוּ מִסִּיבַּת חֶסְרוֹן הַשֶּׁמֶן כִּי הַגּוּף הוּא כְּמוֹ מָשָׁל הַפְּתִילָה וְהָאוֹר הוּא אוֹר הָאֱלֹקִי דְּנִשְׁמַת הָאָדָם שֶׁהוּא כְּמוֹ חִיבּוּר צוּרָה וְחוֹמֶר כַּיָּדוּעַ:

---

heart and mind" and the fact that "it does not last very long" is because the purely *spiritual* excitement has a temporary effect on one's more *earthly* feeling and thinking.

46. The nature of the "oil" in the soul will be described in the following chapter.

47. CHOMER AND TZURAH. Actual physicality ("matter") is created *ex nihilo* from the aspect of *soveiv kol almin* (corresponding to G-d's Will) whereas the qualities and characteristics of created beings ("form") derive from the aspect of *memalei kol almin* (see fn. 77). (See *Derech Mitzvotecha, Tzitzit* ch. 1)

The qualities and characteristics of created beings, i.e., their spiritual dimension, is often referred to as "heaven," whereas their physical component is called "earth."

48. I.e., spiritual with physical, which is difficult and does not last. Thus, one needs oil to create a lasting combination (i.e., a *lamp*, and correspondingly, a lamp within one's soul, as will be explained below).

SUMMARY
OF CHAPTER TWO

The soul contains two "colors" (termed lamp):

1) The *bright radiance*—a G-dly enthusiasm, which is evident when the soul expresses its most sublime sacred attainment, such as in total surrender to G-d when saying "One" in the Shema amid delightful love of G-d. This degree of this radiance is commensurate with the purity of the oil.

2) The *dark radiance*—experiencing G-dly enthusiasm that is comprehensible and physically sensed in one's brain and heart. Here there is a sense of struggle, since occasionally one's negative emotions overpower the G-dly radiance and darken it. But occasionally the G-dly radiance gains the upper hand and transforms one's negative emotions and consumes them. This corresponds to the darker fire, which consumes the wick. Thus, when one is enthusiastically inspired to serve G-d, one's natural heart and brain are inspired as well. However, this sensation soon dissipates for there is a lack of oil, which, as stated earlier, causes the wick to be consumed only gradually.

Hence, both "colors" of flame require (spiritual) oil, which is the theme of the next chapter.

INTRODUCTION TO CHAPTER THREE

Oil represents *chochmah* (wisdom) which, in turn, expresses the theme of selflessness (*bitul*). The selflessness imparted by the oil is required for both aspects of the flame.

The dark flame radiates from the wick, which corresponds to the body and Animal soul. Through the process of self-abnegation and surrender the oil is drawn. Through the smooth flowing of the oil, the dark flame of enthusiasm can burn for a considerable amount of time. If the oil of selflessness does not flow properly, the flame does not last.

At the higher level of the bright flame the oil is also essential. The purity of the radiance of the flame of spirituality depends on the purity of the oil of selflessness. It flows from the highest spiritual levels and brings about a deep, mystical humility.

3.
THE SPIRITUAL EFFECT OF 'OIL'

THE DARK RADIANCE

So the oil is what causes the flame to bond with the wick. This enables the flame to burn a long time and also produces the two colors of white and black flame, as explained above. The same is true regarding the soul and the body. Through the oil, which refers to *chochmah*,[49] the soul bonds with the body in all its faculties,[50] and this bond lasts a long time.

Now, as is known, *chochmah* of the divine soul is termed *koach mah*,[51] "the power of selflessness"—utter abnegation in relation to the divine *ayin*[52] which transcends reason and understanding. Subsequently, *chochmah* spreads its force into *binah*, which represents comprehending something Divine. *Chochmah* and *binah* are the *yud* and the *hey* of the soul,[53] as is known. The potential power in the "spark" in every Jewish soul, even the most lowly, to surrender its self and to be utterly moved before G-dliness, is called *the power of selflessness* of the soul. It is this which is termed "oil"—like oil, which flows in the wick—the body—in order to arouse in it too the quality of abnegation of its sense of ego and its coarseness, so that it should submit and be abnegated and be utterly contrite. This is the abnegation of the self to that which is beyond.

Thus, as we see, sometimes a person's heart will be quelled, leaving its material coarseness. Its free ranging desires will fall away, in the face of intimations of the Living G-d, arousing the person to true *teshuvah* from the inner depth of his heart. This is "the broken and contrite heart."[54] This is from the consumption of the "wick" in the

---

49. The relationship of oil and *chochmah* is determined below in chapter 9.

50. The faculties, or "powers" of the soul and the body, concern the various activities in which one engages, whether of a cerebral or physical nature. Through the effect of "oil," one's active life becomes more spiritual.

51. The word *chochmah* breaks down into the words "*koach mah*" (*Zohar* III:235b), the state of potential that remains undefined—see fn. 5 and next footnote. The potential of *chochmah* is actualized and externalized in *binah*, so that "*chochmah* can be known only through *binah*" (*Tikkunei Zohar, tikkun* 22, p. 63b).

52. The word *ayin* means an exalted spiritual level, the spiritual essence or source of *choch-*

(ג)

וְאָמְנָם סִיבַּת חִיבּוּר וְקֶשֶׁר הָאוֹר בַּפְּתִילָה הוּא הַשֶּׁמֶן לִהְיוֹת הָאוֹר נֶאֱחָז זְמַן רַב כו׳ וְלִהְיוֹת בּוֹ ב׳ גַּוָּונִין דְּלָבָן וְשָׁחוֹר כַּנַ״ל כַּךְ הוּא בִּנְשָׁמָה וְגוּף שֶׁעַל יְדֵי בְּחִינַת הַשֶּׁמֶן שֶׁהוּא בְּחִינַת הַחָכְמָה נַעֲשֶׂה חִיבּוּר הָאוֹר דִּנְשָׁמָה בְּגוּף בְּכָל כּוֹחוֹתֶיהָ בְּקִיּוּם הַדְּלָקָה זְמַן רַב מִטַּעַם הַנַ״ל.

וְהָעִנְיָן הוּא כַּיָּדוּעַ דִּבְחִינַת חָכְמָה שֶׁבַּנֶּפֶשׁ הָאֱלֹקִית הוּא הַנִּקְרָא כֹּחַ מָ״ה וְהוּא בְּחִינַת הַבִּיטּוּל בִּמְצִיאוּת לָאַיִן הָאֱלֹקִי שֶׁלְּמַעְלָה מִן הַטַּעַם וָדַעַת שֶׁאַחַר כַּךְ מִתְפַּשֵּׁט כֹּחָהּ בְּבִינָה שֶׁהִיא הַהַשָּׂגָה הָאֱלֹקִית שֶׁהֵן י״ה שֶׁבַּנְּשָׁמָה כַּיָּדוּעַ וְהַיְינוּ מַה שֶּׁיֵּשׁ בְּכֹחַ וּבְהֶעְלֵם בְּכָל נִיצוֹץ קָטָן מִיִּשְׂרָאֵל לְהִתְבַּטֵּל וְלָזוּז מִמְּקוֹמָן לְגַמְרֵי לְגַבֵּי אֱלֹקוּת נִקְרָא כֹּחַ מָה שֶׁבַּנְּשָׁמָה וְזֶהוּ הַנִּקְרָא שֶׁמֶן כְּמוֹ הַשֶּׁמֶן שֶׁנִּמְשָׁךְ אַחַר הַפְּתִילָה שֶׁהוּא הַגּוּף לְעוֹרֵר בּוֹ גַּם כֵּן בְּחִינַת הַבִּיטּוּל שֶׁל יֵשׁוּתוֹ וְגַסּוּתוֹ לִהְיוֹת נִכְנָע וּבָטֵל וְנִשְׁבָּר לְגַמְרֵי שֶׁנִּקְרָא בִּיטּוּל הַיֵּשׁ לָאַיִן.

כְּמוֹ שֶׁאָנוּ רוֹאִים שֶׁפִּתְאוֹם יִכָּנַע לֵב הַחוּמְרִי מִגַּסּוּת שֶׁלּוֹ וְיִפּוֹל תַּאֲוַת שְׁרִירוּת לִבּוֹ לְגַבֵּי אֱלֹקִים חַיִּים לְעוֹרְרוֹ בִּתְשׁוּבָה שְׁלֵימָה מְקִירַת הַלֵּב וְהוּא הַנִּקְרָא לֵב נִשְׁבָּר

---

mah, as in the verse (Job 28:12), "From where will wisdom come," translated by Kabbalah to connote that *ayin* is the spiritual essence or source of *chochmah*, and that "*Chochmah* appears from *ayin*," for *chochmah* appears from nothingness (*ayin*) and continually reverts to nothingness. For this reason it is compared to a flash of lightning, since it constantly flashes in and out of existence. This is also why *chochmah* breaks down into *koach mah*, as explained in the previous footnote.

Literally, *ayin* means "nothing" as in the depiction of Creation as *yesh me'ayin*, "something from nothing"—*creatio ex nihilo*.

53. See chapter 1 above.

54. Psalms 51:19.

Divine radiance by means of the oil, on account of the power of *mah* (selflessness) which it imparts.

This "selflessness" is due to good oil, which flows properly in the wick. If it does not flow properly then the Divine radiance does not cleave to one's mind and physical emotions and it is quickly extinguished.

Thus, this [good] oil causes the burning of the dark color of the flame,[55] the "flame of Y-H." Gradually this flame consumes the wick, i.e. the body, so that it too should be absorbed in the Divine radiance, the radiance of spiritual ecstasy, with flames of longing, lasting a long time.

BRIGHT RADIANCE

The second effect[56] of the oil is the clarity of the higher "white" flame of the soul which is called *bright radiance.*[57] This depends on the purity of the oil, which is drawn into and consumed by the flame.

This [double effect] is because the power of selflessness—termed "oil"—has two levels. The first is the way it flows from concealment to revelation. This causes the quelling and abnegation of the [material] self before G-d,[58] within the actual body, so that in his very physicality the person has a contrite spirit.

The second level relates to the manner that the power of selflessness is manifested at its root, in the actual divine *ayin*, as it is written "*chochmah* appears from *ayin*," literally from the spiritual level of *ayin.* For every soul contains a quality of utter abnegation before G-dliness, to become *ayin*, literally "nothing," and not just to transcend one's *physical self.* This is a kind of intense meekness and humility in the very essence of one's being, until one's soul is really "as dust to all,"[59] not feeling any importance in oneself at all in everything one does. (This is called in Yiddish "*nishtkayt, er is gor nisht be'etzem*" [nothingness, he is utterly nothing].)

---

55. I.e., the oil causes the flame to burn properly.

56. See above chapter 1, that there are two effects of a well-structured lamp: One that the wick burns well and lasts a long time; the second, that it produces a bright, radiant light. After having explained the first effect in terms of the human soul, the author now proceeds to explain the second effect in a similar vein.

וְנִדְכֶּה כו׳ שֶׁזֶּהוּ כִּלְיוֹן הַפְּתִילָה בָּאוֹר הָאֱלֹקִי עַל יְדֵי הַשֶּׁמֶן דְּכֹחַ מָה שֶׁנִּמְשָׁךְ כו׳.

וְהַיְינוּ שֶׁמֶן טוֹב שֶׁנִּמְשָׁךְ הֵיטֵב בַּפְּתִילָה כַּנַ״ל וְאִם אֵינוֹ נִמְשָׁךְ הֵיטֵב אָז הָאוֹר אֱלֹקִי אֵינוֹ נֶאֱחָז בַּשֵּׂכֶל וּמִדּוֹת הַגּוּפְנִים וְקוֹפֵץ מִיָּד וּמִסְתַּלֵּק כַּנַ״ל.

וְנִמְצָא שֶׁשֶּׁמֶן הַזֶּה זֶהוּ הַגּוֹרֵם דְּלִיקַת גַּוָּון הָאוֹר הַשָּׁחוֹר שֶׁנִּקְרָא שַׁלְהֶבֶת יָ־הּ הַנַ״ל הַשּׂוֹרֵף וּמְכַלֶּה מְעַט מְעַט לַפְּתִילָה שֶׁהוּא הַגּוּף לִיכָּלֵל גַּם הוּא בָּאוֹר הָאֱלֹקִי שֶׁהוּא אוֹר הִתְפַּעֲלוּת אֱלֹקוּת בְּרִשְׁפֵּי אֵשׁ הַתְּשׁוּקָה שֶׁנִּקְרָא שַׁלְהֶבֶת יָ־הּ כַּנַ״ל וִימַשֵּׁךְ זְמַן רַב לֹא יִכָּבֶה כְּלָל וְדַי לַמֵּבִין.

וְתוֹעֶלֶת הַב׳ מִן הַשֶּׁמֶן זֶה הוּא בְּהִירוּת הָאוֹר הַלָּבָן הָעֶלְיוֹן שֶׁבַּנְּשָׁמָה שֶׁנִּקְרָא נְהוֹרָא חִוְּורָא שֶׁהוּא לְפִי צְלִילַת הַשֶּׁמֶן מִפְּנֵי שֶׁכָּלֶה וְנִשְׁאָב הַשֶּׁמֶן בָּאוֹר הַמּוֹשֵׁךְ אוֹתוֹ כַּנַ״ל.

הָעִנְיָן הוּא כַּיָּדוּעַ שֶׁכֹּחַ מָה זֶה הַנִּקְרָא שֶׁמֶן יֵשׁ בּוֹ ב׳ מַדְרֵגוֹת הָא׳ כְּמוֹ שֶׁבָּא וְנִמְשָׁךְ מִן הַהֶעְלֵם לַגִּילּוּי שֶׁזֶּהוּ הָעוֹשֶׂה הַהַכְנָעָה וּבִיטּוּל הַיֵּשׁ לְאַיִן גַּם בַּגּוּף לִהְיוֹת לוֹ רוּחַ נִשְׁבָּרָה בְּגַשְׁמִיּוּתוֹ כַּנַ״ל.

וְהַב׳ הוּא כְּמוֹ שֶׁבְּחִינַת כֹּחַ מָ״ה זֶה הוּא בְּשָׁרְשׁוֹ בִּבְחִינַת אַיִן הָאֱלֹקִי מַמָּשׁ כְּמוֹ שֶׁכָּתוּב וְהַחָכְמָה מֵאַיִן תִּמָּצֵא מֵאַיִן מַמָּשׁ וְהוּא מַה שֶּׁבְּכָל נְשָׁמָה יֵשׁ בְּחִינַת בִּיטּוּל עַצְמִי לֶאֱלֹקוּת לִהְיוֹת בִּבְחִינַת אַיִן מַמָּשׁ וְלֹא לַעֲשׂוֹת בִּיטּוּל הַיֵּשׁ לְבַד כו׳ כַּיָּדוּעַ שֶׁזֶּהוּ כְּמוֹ עִנְיַן הַשִּׁפְלוּת וְהָעֲנָוָה הַיְתֵירָה בְּעֶצֶם מַהוּתוֹ עַד שֶׁנַּפְשׁוֹ כֶּעָפָר לַכֹּל תִּהְיֶה מַמָּשׁ בִּלְתִּי מַרְגִּישׁ בְּעַצְמוֹ שׁוּם דְּבַר מַעֲלָה כְּלָל וּכְלָל בְּכֹל אֲשֶׁר עוֹשֶׂה כו׳ (וְנִקְרָא בִּלְשׁוֹן אִידִישׁ נִישְׁטִקַייט עֶר אִיז גָאר נִישְׁט בְּעֶצֶם כו׳).

---

57. Lit., "white radiance."

58. Lit., *ayin*, the Divine "nothingness" beyond all existence, termed "nothing" as it is incomprehensible to man. See footnote 52.

59. Liturgy, end of the Amidah.

This is the meaning of the verse "in the heart of every wise of heart, I have placed *chochmah*,"[60] and "He gives *chochmah* to the wise,"[61] and "let my soul be as dust"; [by which] certainly and spontaneously [will be fulfilled the request[59]] "open my heart to Your Torah."[62]

THE POWER OF HUMILITY

It is through this humility that man elicits the supernal radiance of the inwardness of *chochmah*,[63] revealing the radiance of *Ein Sof*,[64] which shines from the concealment of the Essence[65] [which is] in each soul, with the quality of the very essence of the light. This is the light sown for the Supernal *tzaddik*, mentioned above,[66] and is called *bright radiance*, which shines with the ecstasy of one's whole essence expressing *ahava b'tanugim* with *kelot hanefesh*.[67] Another mode of expression might be that of *teshuvah* with true self-sacrifice.[68]

This [humility] derives from the consumption of the oil, from the fact that it is drawn into the flame, [thereby expressing] lowliness and humility,[69] for the upper flame draws the oil [and consumes it, which in human terms] enables one to reach the essential *ayin* of G-dliness. This causes the brightness of the upper flame—due to the purity of the oil, which is a manifestation of the depths of true lowliness and humility, not being conscious of one's own self at all in any way.

Thus, deeply hidden in the inner quality of *koach mah*[70] [deriving from the "oil"], are the two kinds of radiance of the flame, the bright radiance and the dark radiance. By means of selflessness they emerge from concealment to be revealed in the soul.[71]

---

60. Exodus 31:6.

61. Daniel 2:21.

62. All these quotations imply that through each person attaining a level of *chochmah* and selflessness, G-d grants yet more intense levels of spiritual humility and access to Torah knowledge.

63. I.e., the essence of *chochmah*.

64. EIN SOF: Lit. "Infinite," "Endless," meaning the most absolute Infinite force of G-d, totally beyond description, knowledge, and comprehension, completely beyond any boundaries; the Essence of G-d Himself, the innermost aspect of the innermost level of *keter*. *Keter* (Will) is the intermediary between the *Ein Sof* and the *sefirot*.

65. The more inner level is "concealment," but it is expressed through revelation of light.

66. In the beginning of chapter 2.

וְהוּא מַה שֶּׁכָּתוּב וּבְלֵב כָּל חֲכַם לֵב נָתַתִּי חָכְמָה כו׳ וְכֵן יָהֵיב חָכְמְתָא לְחַכִּימִין וְכֵן מַה שֶּׁאוֹמְרִים וְנַפְשִׁי כֶּעָפָר כו׳ אָז וַדַּאי פְּתַח לִבִּי בְּתוֹרָתֶיךָ מִמֵּילָא.

שֶׁעַל יְדֵי זֶה הוּא הַגּוֹרֵם לְהַמְשִׁיךְ בְּחִינַת אוֹר הָעֶלְיוֹן דִּפְנִימִית חָכְמָה שֶׁזֶּהוּ גִּלּוּי אוֹר אֵין סוֹף שֶׁבָּא וּמֵאִיר מִן הֶעְלֵם הָעַצְמוּת בְּכָל נְשָׁמָה בִּבְחִינַת עַצְמִיּוּת הָאוֹר שֶׁזֶּהוּ אוֹר זָרוּעַ לְצַדִּיק עֶלְיוֹן הַנַּ״ל שֶׁנִּקְרָא נְהוֹרָא חִוְּורָא אוֹר הַמֵּאִיר בִּבְחִינַת הִתְפַּעֲלוּת כָּל הָעַצְמִיּוּת בְּאַהֲבָה רַבָּה בַּתַּעֲנוּגִים בִּכְלוֹת הַנֶּפֶשׁ אוֹ בִּתְשׁוּבָה בִּמְסִירַת נֶפֶשׁ מַמָּשׁ.

וְזֶהוּ מִצַּד כִּלְיוֹן הַשֶּׁמֶן זֶה שֶׁנִּשְׁאָב בָּאוֹר כו׳ שֶׁהוּא כְּמוֹ הַשִּׁפְלוּת וַעֲנָוָה כו׳ דְּאוֹר הָעֶלְיוֹן מוֹשֵׁךְ אוֹתוֹ דְּהַיְינוּ שֶׁיִּהְיֶה בִּבְחִינַת אַיִן הָעַצְמִי שֶׁבֵּאלֹקוּת וְזֶהוּ הָעוֹשֶׂה בְּהִירוּת הָאוֹר הָעֶלְיוֹן לְפִי צְלִילַת הַשֶּׁמֶן שֶׁהוּא עוֹמֶק אֲמִתִּית הַשִּׁפְלוּת וְהָעֲנָוָה בְּהֶעְדֵּר הַרְגָּשַׁת עַצְמוֹ מִכֹּל וָכֹל כו׳.

הֲרֵי הָיָה בְּכֹחַ מָ״ה זֶה כָּלוּל בְּהֶעְלֵם גָּדוֹל ב׳ גַּוְונֵי אוֹר הַלָּלוּ דִּנְהוֹרָא חִוְּורָא וּנְהוֹרָא אוּכָּמָא וְעַל יָדוֹ יָצְאוּ מִן הַהֶעְלֵם לְגִילּוּי בַּנְּשָׁמָה וְדַי לַמֵּבִין.

---

67. See footnotes 33-34.

68. The upper, bright flame shines with an intense radiance that might either be the expression of intense delightful love of G-d, or an equally intense mood of *teshuvah*, returning to G-d with a sense of dedicated personal surrender.

69. The lower, dark flame consumes the wick, expressing one's going beyond materialistic desires. In the upper flame it is the oil which is consumed—producing a brighter light—expressing a movement of conscious humility, as the author proceeds to explain.

70. See footnote 51.

71. Hence, the function of the two levels: the lower, dark radiance enables one to transcend physical desires, whereas the upper bright radiance expresses the feeling of genuine humility before the Essential G-dly *Ayin*.

(The same is understood of the "general soul"[72]—*malchut* of *Atzilut* which also has two kinds of radiance. As it says in the *Zohar*,[73] explaining the verse "G-d, do not be silent,"[74] that the lower radiance calls continuously to the higher radiance.[75] This is sufficient for the wise.)

72. See footnote 24.

73. I:77b. *Zohar* (lit. "radiance"): basic work of Kabbalah; compiled by Rabbi Shimon Bar Yochai (second century Mishnaic sage); written in Hebrew and Aramaic as a commentary on the Torah.

74. Psalms 83:2.

75. Thus there is a parallel between the individual person's soul with its two kinds of spiritual radiance, and the "general Soul" of *malchut*, with *its* two kinds of radiance.

The Divine radiance which is within existence, giving it life (*memalei kol almin*),

(וְכַךְ יוּבַן בַּנְּשָׁמָה הַכְּלָלִית שֶׁזֶּהוּ בְּחִינַת מַלְכוּת
דַּאֲצִילוּת בְּב׳ גַּוְונֵי אוֹר הַנַּ״ל כְּמוֹ שֶׁכָּתוּב בַּזֹּהַר בְּפֵירוּשׁ
אֱלֹקִים אַל דֳּמִי לָךְ דִּנְהוֹרָא תַּתָּאָה קָארֵי תָּדִיר לִנְהוֹרָא
עִילָּאָה כו׳ וְדַי לַמֵּבִין:)

"calls" to the transcendent Divine radiance which is beyond (*sovev kol almin*), seeking to be united with it.

Ahavat Olam, (lit. eternal love) also connotes "love of the world," i.e., a form of love of G-d that occurs by way of the concealment of the G-dly energy within the worlds—*memalei kol almin*. This energy constantly ascends amid tremendous yearning to unite with its source—*sovev kol almin*.

Man too, when he contemplates the concealment of the G-dly energy, is aroused with tremendous yearning to the *Or Hachaim* (Light of life, i.e., G-d). This love is called "animal," for it comes from within the world (—"it is lowly"). (*Likkutei Torah, Ekev,* 13c)

SUMMARY OF CHAPTER THREE

The operation of a well-structured lamp requires oil. The same applies to the soul. In order to attain any sort of G-dly inspiration, whether the sublime stage of self-surrender in delightful love, or the transformation of negative emotions to focus on G-dliness, one must use spiritual oil. Oil refers to *chochmah* of the G-dly soul, which itself expresses the theme of *bittul* (selflessness), and is concealed within the *binah*, the G-dly comprehension in the soul. This causes the body to subjugate itself to G-dliness as well.

We observe empirically that one's corporeal heart can suddenly experience complete subjugation when the person understands a Divine reality. This arouses the person to total *teshuvah*. He is then termed "broken-hearted" (Psalms 51:19) and all self-importance he may possesss immediately dissolves. This is caused by healthy oil, which is drawn after the wick. When the oil is of inferior quality, the wick is unable to absorb it and is swiftly consumed.

The second (aforementioned) benefit resulting from the oil is the emergence of a pure flame, or radiance. In human terms, this refers to the essential light of the soul.

Thus, the two levels of the oil of the soul—*chochmah*, selflessness—correspond to the two aforementioned benefits of a well-structured lamp:

1) Abnegation of the "self" of the body— paralleling *the darker radiance* which depicts the flame's cleaving to the wick and gradual consumption; 2) Essential abnegation of the soul, also sensed by the body (termed "wick" or *chomer*, "matter") to illuminate with a sensation of "may my soul be as dust," "giving wisdom to the wise" (i.e., selflessness to those who sense it)—paralleling *the illuminating radiance* that results from healthy oil.

Hence, these two colors are present in G-dly comprehension, which in turn, reveals them (similar to oil, which, as mentioned earlier, contains the two colors of the flame).

INTRODUCTION TO CHAPTER FOUR

The two aspects of the flame relate to two kinds of *hitbonenut*, contemplation in prayer. This chapter presents the system of the "lower" contemplation focusing on the Divine Radiance that fills all worlds. This method of contemplation is described via a commentary on Psalm 145, *Ashrei*, a prayer that plays an important role in *Pesukei d'Zimra* ("Verses of Praise") of the Morning Service.

Chasidic teachings speak of two aspects of the Divine: *Memalei kol almin*—the Divine Radiance filling all worlds, and *sovev kol almin*—that which surrounds all worlds.

By focusing on the lower radiance, the worshipper seeks to elevate it and thereby unite it with the more exalted level of radiance. This elevation takes place through song, the melodious process of prayer. The worshipper bears in mind that at the same time the angels and souls are also singing in the upper worlds with the same goal. When the unification takes place, a stream of blessing pours forth from the highest levels to the lowest, flowing through all the worlds.

The worshipper serves as the agent for this cosmic spiritual interaction.

4.
CONTEMPLATING YICHUDA TATA'AH

In order to better understand all of the above, let us first consider the well-known idea that there are two kinds of contemplation. The first is the subject of G-d's Oneness as it appears from man's perspective,[76] which is the level of *memalei kol almin*,[77] and the aspect of *Baruch shem k'vod malchuto l'olam vaed* [Blessed be the Name of the glory of His kingship for ever],[78] which is in the level of the Divine Name *Elokim*.[79] (This corresponds to the lower radiance, also termed the "dark radiance" mentioned above—as relating to the individual soul, created in the Divine Form.[80])

The second is contemplating the subject of G-d's Oneness as it appears from G-d's perspective,[81] of *sovev kol almin*,[82] of *Havaya*,

---

76. *Yichuda tata'ah* in the Hebrew.

YICHUDA ILA'AH - YICHUDA TATA'AH. The *Zohar* I:18b states that the verse *Shema Yisrael Hashem Elokeinu Hashem Echad* represents *yichuda ila'ah* (the higher unity) whereas *Baruch Shem Kevod Malchuto Le'olam Va'ed* represents *yichuda tata'ah* (the lower unity).

Yichuda ila'ah is the unity of G-d within Himself as He is in His essence, completely transcending all worlds. The creation of the worlds from absolute nothing does not cause any change in His Unity (and certainly not in His Essence), so that He remains the only being after their creation, just as He was before they were created, when there was nothing at all besides Him. As such all of existence, including the very highest worlds, is absolutely nothing, as if null and void.

Yichuda tata'ah is the unity of G-d as He is manifested within the world. It is the perception of His unity from the point of view of the worlds as He creates and enlivens them. From this perspective, even though the worlds actually exist, nevertheless, their entire existence and life-force is nothing other than the Ten Utterances which create and enliven them. As such, their existence is entirely dependent upon Him.

Yichuda tata'ah is the view that should prevail in our Divine service: firstly, because we must be honest with ourselves and realize our limited spiritual vision, and secondly, because G-d's intent in creating the world is that the world should recognize G-dliness within its own context.

Nevertheless, *yichuda tata'ah* does not raise a person above the world's limited frame of reference. So a person must have a taste of *yichuda ila'ah*, so as to weaken his material disposition and strengthen his higher self. See *Kuntres Etz Chaim* (English translation) pp. 46-62.

77. MEMALEI—SOVEV. *Memalei kol almin* is immanent Divine energy. It permeates all of creation and is mutually interactive and interresponsive with the subject that it enlivens. By way of analogy, the life force of the soul is clothed within the body in a way that changes the body fundamentally. It is not simply life-force which enlivens the body; it is the life force of *the body*, making the person a live person rather than a dead one. (See *Sefer HaMaamarim 5703*, p. 31) For *Sovev kol almin* see footnote 82.

78. *Pesachim* 56a. The second verse of the Shema.

(ד)

וְהִנֵּה לְהָבִין כָּל זֶה בְּבֵיאוּר יוֹתֵר הִנֵּה יֵשׁ לְהַקְדִּים הַיָּדוּעַ שֶׁיֵּשׁ ב׳ מִינֵי הִתְבּוֹנְנוּת הָא׳ בִּבְחִינַת יִחוּדָא תַּתָּאָה שֶׁהוּא בְּחִינַת מְמַלֵּא כָּל עָלְמִין שֶׁהוּא עִנְיַן בָּרוּךְ שֵׁם כְּבוֹד מַלְכוּתוֹ לְעוֹלָם וָעֶד כַּיָּדוּעַ שֶׁהוּא בִּבְחִינַת שֵׁם אֱלֹקִים (וְהַיְינוּ בְּחִינַת נְהוֹרָא תַּתָּאָה הַנַּ״ל בִּנְשָׁמָה פְּרָטִית שֶׁהִיא בְּצֶלֶם אֱלֹקִים וְנִקְרָא נְהוֹרָא אוּכָּמָא כו׳).

וְהַב׳ בִּבְחִינַת יִחוּדָא עִילָּאָה דִּבְחִינַת סוֹבֵב כָּל עָלְמִין בְּשֵׁם הוי״ה שֶׁזֶּהוּ עִנְיַן שְׁמַע יִשְׂרָאֵל (וְהוּא בְּחִינַת נְהוֹרָא

---

79. ELOKIM. All of the Names of G-d found in the Torah are representative of a certain type of action. When Moses wished to know G-d's Name, He replied, "My Name you wish to know? According to My deeds I am called" (*Shemot Rabbah* 3:5, 6). Kabbalah describes how the Divine Names corresponds to the *sefirot*: *E-l* corresponds to *chesed*; *Elokim* to *gevurah*, etc.

Elokim is associated with "judgment" (limitation, restriction and the laws of nature). It is thus associated with time and space, which essentially derive from *Malchut.* Thus, *Elokim* shares the same numerical value as the Hebrew words for nature (*hateva*).

The relationship between the two Names *Havaya* and *Elokim* is expressed in the verse (*Psalms* 84:12), "For *Havaya*, *Elokim* (L-rd, G-d), is a sun and a shield..." Metaphorically, *Havaya* is the sun and *Elokim* the (sun's) shield. *Havaya* is associated with "mercy" (unlimited and transcendent revelation), and with the Hebrew words for past, present, and future *haya, hoveh, v'yihyeh*—referring to a realm where the three exist simultaneously (*Zohar* III:257b in *Raya Mehemna*). *Havaya* thus represents that which transcends the limitations of time and space.

80. The soul therefore is a microcosm, with two kinds of radiance that parallel the two kinds of radiance in the macrocosm.

81. *Yichuda ila'ah* in the Hebrew. See footnote 76.

82. *Sovev kol almin* is the Divine energy that transcends creation, while *memalei kol almin* is the Divine energy invested within the creation. *Sovev* acts in a remote, imperative, unidirectional manner (i.e., from above to below, but not vice versa).

An analogy: Sunlight shines into a room and illuminates it. However, the room itself is not changed thereby, since the light emanates from a source outside of the room. It is not the room itself that lights up. Even when the light illuminates the room, the walls of the room do not actually absorb the light. The light is merely there; but as light—an illumination from the luminary. It does not become part of that which it illuminates. Similarly, the energy of *sovev* is of an infinite order that cannot be confined within limited creatures. It therefore "encompasses" them in a pervasive and transcending form. This is why it is called *makif*; it is "there," but remains remote from the object it illuminates. (See *Tanya* ch. 48; *Sefer HaMaamarim 5703*, p. 31).

which is the aspect of Shema Yisrael[83] (termed earlier as *Supernal Radiance*, the bright radiance, sown for the supernal *tzaddik*).

EXPLANATION OF PSALM 145:1 (ASHREI): 1. THE NAME ELOKIM

This is explained elsewhere[84] on the verse "I will exalt You, my G-d [*Elokei*], the King"[85]: This refers to *malchut* of *Atzilut*, the source of all the worlds, which is expressed in the name *Elokim*. *Elokim* implies power and mastery, like in the verses "and the powerful ones [*eyley*] of the land"[86] and "their claims should come to *Elokim*,"[87] meaning to the Judge [master]. And both these qualities [of power and mastery] are unified above in "the Living G-d and eternal King,"[88] i.e., in the power and the Divine radiance which bring all that exists into being *ex nihilo*. This is the power of the Divine life-force, active in that which is created.[89]

Hence G-d is called "*Elokay haElokim*" (G-d of spiritual forces),[90] meaning that He is the power and source of all divine forces. These are termed *Bnei haElokim*, "children of *Elokim*," which are the angels,[91] intermediary divine powers imbued with individual spiritual radiance. They emerge from the divine *ayin* and enter the realm of created existence. Thus G-d is called the G-d of these forces. The Gentiles too term Him "*Elokay haElokim*."[92]

The same is regarding [the concept of mastery] expressed in the Divine Name A-D-N-Y,[93] He Who is known as Master over all,[94] as

---

83. Deuteronomy 6:4. Thus, it is referring to the first line of the Shema as distinct from the second.

84. *Torah Or* 40c.

85. Psalms 145:1 (*Ashrei*). This verse continues, "and I will bless Your Name for ever and ever." The rest of this chapter comprises a commentary on *Ashrei* and other passages in the morning liturgy.

86. II Kings 24:15.

87. Exodus 22:8.

88. Liturgy, blessings before the Shema.

89. KOACH HAPOEL B'NIFAL: The activating force of the Creator which much continuously be in the thing created to give it life and existence.

Nehemiah 9:6 states, "You give life to them all": G-d's energy in every created being not only gives it life and vivifies it, but continuously brings it into existence *ex nihilo*. The verse is thus interpreted, for the phrase "to give life" does not necessary imply "to create"—as, for example, the soul which gives life to and vivifies the body, yet does not bring it into being. Whereas in Creation the energy not only vivifies but also creates and must continuously flow into the created being, for without it, it would revert to nothingness; by giving life, He actually creates it *ex nihilo*. Hence,

עִילָּאָה הַנַּ״ל שֶׁנִּקְרָא נְהוֹרָא חִיוְּורָא כו׳ אוֹר זָרוּעַ לְצַדִּיק עֶלְיוֹן כו׳).

וּבֵיאוּר הָעִנְיָן יָדוּעַ וּמְבוֹאָר בְּמָקוֹם אַחֵר עַל פָּסוּק אֲרוֹמִמְךָ אֱלֹקַי הַמֶּלֶךְ שֶׁזֶּהוּ בְּחִינַת מַלְכוּת דַּאֲצִילוּת מְקוֹר כָּל הָעוֹלָמוֹת שֶׁנִּקְרָא בְּשֵׁם אֱלֹקִים דַּוְקָא וְכַיָּדוּעַ בְּפֵירוּשׁ שֵׁם אֱלֹקִים לְשׁוֹן כֹּחַ וְאַדְנוּת כְּמוֹ וְאֵלֵי הָאָרֶץ כו׳ וּכְמוֹ עַד הָאֱלֹקִים יָבֹא שֶׁהוּא הַשּׁוֹפֵט כו׳ וּשְׁנֵיהֶם אֶחָד לְמַעְלָה בֵּאלֹקִים חַיִּים וּמֶלֶךְ עוֹלָם שֶׁהוּא בְּחִינַת הַכֹּחַ וְאוֹר אֱלֹקִי הַמְהַוֶּוה כָּל הַנִּמְצָאִים מֵאַיִן לְיֵשׁ וְנִקְרָא כֹּחַ הַפּוֹעֵל אֱלֹקִי בַּנִּפְעָל.

וּלְכַךְ נִקְרָא אֱלֹקֵי הָאֱלֹקִים כְּלוֹמַר כֹּחַ וּמְקוֹר כָּל כּוֹחוֹת הָאֱלֹקִים שֶׁנִּקְרָאִים בְּנֵי הָאֱלֹקִים שֶׁהֵן הַמַּלְאָכִים שֶׁהֵמָּה כֹּחוֹת אֱלֹקִים אֶמְצָעִים בְּחֵלֶק וְהֶאָרָה דְּהֶאָרָה פְּרָטִית שֶׁנִּמְצָאִים מֵאַיִן הָאֱלֹקִי לְיֵשׁ וְזֶהוּ שֶׁנִּקְרָא אֱלֹקֵי הָאֱלֹקִים וְגַם אוּמּוֹת הָעוֹלָם קָרוּ לֵיהּ אֱלָקָא דֶּאֱלָקַיָּיא כו׳.

וְהַיְינוּ גַּם כֵּן שֵׁם אדני דְּאִשְׁתְּמוֹדַע אָדוֹן עַל כּוֹלָּא כְּמוֹ

He constantly renews the existence of the world and all the creatures, creating them anew from nothing at every moment, just as in the beginning of Creation. So, in reality, "to give life" and to "bring into being" are identical.

90. Deuteronomy 10:17. *Midrash Hagadol*, *Moreh Nevuchim* 3:6 and *Ramban* translate this phrase as "G-d of the angels." This complies with "children of angels" below.

91. See Job 2:1. Scripture calls the angels "*Elokim*," as in "For the L-rd your G-d is the G-d of G-ds (*Elokim*)..." and "Praise the G-d of G-ds (*Elokim*)..." and the sons of G-d (*Elokim*) came to present themselves..." They derive their nurture from the external of the life-force, which is merely the state of letters. Similarly the name *Elokim* is an external state compared to *Havaya*. (*Iggeret haTeshuvah*, chapter 4.)

92. *Menachot* 110a.

93. ADNAI: There are many Hebrew names for G-d in Scripture, each of which expresses a different aspect or attribute of the Divinity. The name comprised of the four letters A-D-N-Y, pronounced in conversation as *Adnai*, is from the Hebrew word *adnut*, mastery, and refers to G-d as the Master of all works.

94. *Tikkunei Zohar,* Introduction 17b.

the phrase, "Almighty G-d is the master (*Adon*) over all works,"[95] and the verse, "great is our Master, and [with] immense power."[96] This is the second aspect of the Name *Elokim*, the concept of a Judge,[97] as in the verse, "Will the Judge of the whole world not work justice?",[98] which implies sovereignty and kingship. (And similarly the verse, "you are a Prince of *Elokim*").[99]

2. KINGSHIP

Both [these themes of power and kingship] are one. For *malchut*, which is the lowest aspect of the ten *sefirot* of *Atzilut*, is the first source of the coming into being of all the worlds and creatures *ex nihilo*, as in the verse, "Your Kingship is a kingship over all worlds, and Your dominion is throughout all generations."[100]

We can compare this quality with human kingship: Kingship is only an external aura, spreading from the essence of the king, insofar that his reign and his power extend over his people. This aura of kingship is not considered an inner quality of his being, like the faculty of love or of wisdom. Thus the verse states "G-d is King; He has garbed Himself with grandeur."[101] He is "robed" and veiled[102] to be King over the worlds, for this quality of kingship is only an external garment.

3. EXALTING THE ASPECT ELOKIM

Despite this [apparently secondary nature of kingship], King David said "I will exalt You, my G-d (*Elokei*), the King." *Elokei* signifies the name *Elokim*, the Divine life-force active in that which is created, i.e., *memale kol almin*. And "I will exalt You, [actual] *Elokei*, the King," for even though this quality of *malchut* is only an external aura, its root is very exalted, namely *keter malchut*.[103]

---

95. Liturgy, Shabbat morning.

96. Psalms 147:5.

97. The first aspect is *power and mastery*, and the second is that of *judge*.

98. Genesis 18:25.

99. Ibid. 23:6. Ramban on 23:19 comments that this term expresses leadership and mastery.

100. Psalms 145:13.

101. Ibid. 93:1.

שֶׁאוֹמְרִים אֵל אָדוֹן עַל כָּל כו׳ וְזֶהוּ גָּדוֹל אֲדוֹנֵינוּ וְרַב כֹּחַ כו׳ שֶׁזֶּהוּ עִנְיַן הַב׳ בֵּאלֹקִים לְשׁוֹן שׁוֹפֵט כְּמוֹ שֶׁכָּתוּב הֲשׁוֹפֵט כָּל הָאָרֶץ כו׳ וְהוּא בְּחִינַת שְׂרָרָה וּמַלְכוּת (כְּמוֹ נְשִׂיא אֱלֹקִים אַתָּה כו׳).

וְהַכֹּל אֶחָד מִשּׁוּם דְּבִבְחִינַת מַלְכוּת שֶׁהוּא בְּחִינָה הָאַחֲרוֹנָה דְּעֶשֶׂר סְפִירוֹת דַּאֲצִילוּת הוּא הַמָּקוֹר הָרִאשׁוֹן לְהִתְהַוּוּת כָּל הָעוֹלָמוֹת וְהַבְּרוּאִים מֵאַיִן לְיֵשׁ וּכְמוֹ שֶׁכָּתוּב מַלְכוּתְךָ מַלְכוּת כָּל עוֹלָמִים וּמֶמְשַׁלְתְּךָ כו׳.

וְעַל דֶּרֶךְ מָשָׁל מַלְכוּתָא דְּאַרְעָא שֶׁמִּדָּה זוֹ אֵינָהּ רַק הִתְפַּשְּׁטוּת חִצוֹנִיּוּת מֵעַצְמוּתוֹ שֶׁמִּתְפַּשֵּׁט מַלְכוּתוֹ וּמֶמְשַׁלְתּוֹ עַל עַמּוֹ כו׳ וְאֵין זֶה נֶחְשָׁב מִכּוֹחוֹת הָעַצְמִיִּים כְּמִדַּת כֹּחַ הָאַהֲבָה וְכֹחַ הַחָכְמָה כַּיָּדוּעַ וְזֶהוּ שֶׁכָּתוּב ה׳ מָלָךְ גֵּאוּת לָבֵשׁ שֶׁנִּתְלַבֵּשׁ וְנִתְצַמְצֵם לִהְיוֹת מֶלֶךְ עַל הָעוֹלָמוֹת לְפִי שֶׁאֵינָהּ אֶלָּא בְּחִינַת לְבוּשׁ חִיצוֹנִי לְבַד כו׳.

וְעַל כָּל זֶה אָמַר דָּוִד אֲרוֹמִמְךָ אֱלֹקַי הַמֶּלֶךְ פֵּירוּשׁ אֱלֹקַי הוּא בְּחִינַת שֵׁם אֱלֹקִים כֹּחַ הַפּוֹעֵל אֱלֹקִי בַּנִּפְעָל בְּחִינַת מְמַלֵּא כָּל עָלְמִין הַנַּ״ל שֶׁנִּקְרָא אֱלֹקַי מַמָּשׁ אֲרוֹמִמְךָ אֱלֹקַי הַמֶּלֶךְ אַף עַל פִּי שֶׁאֵין זֶה רַק הֶאָרָה חִצוֹנִיּוּת דִּבְחִינַת הַמַּלְכוּת כַּנַּ״ל אֲבָל שָׁרְשׁוֹ הוּא הַגְּבֵהַּ לְמַעְלָה וְהוּא בְּחִינַת כֶּתֶר מַלְכוּת.

---

102. TZIMTZUM: Lit. "contracted." See fn. 110.

103. Lit., the Crown of Kingship. *Keter* is the highest *sefirah,* whereas *malchut* is the lowest. "*Malchut* is rooted in *keter*" refers not to the regular level of *keter,* but to an extremely lofty level of *keter—keter malchut,* the first aspect of *malchut* following *ze'er anpin* as the *sefirot* descend. Elsewhere, Chasidut implies that *keter malchut* is the essence of *atik* (inner *keter*). The fact that this transcendent level is manifested in the lowest of the *sefirot* is in accordance with the rule that the higher the source, the lower the revelation.

4. THE KING ALONE, BEYOND

[The exalted level of *keter malchut*] implies the level of G-dly exaltedness which emanates solely from Himself. At this level He is called "the King who is exalted alone,"[104] completely beyond that [lower] level at which G-d is called King over the worlds and created things. This [higher level] is *malchut* of *Atzilut*[105] as it is purely within *Atzilut* (and this is signified by the large *daled* of the word *Echad* [One], in the Shema[106]).

5. UNIFICATION

The verse ["I will exalt You"] is saying that even *Elokim*, the Divine life-force within the worlds, shall be exalted higher and higher so as to be at the level of "the King," termed "the King who is exalted alone."[107] This is the unification of *memale kol almin* with *sovev kol almin.*

This unification is also expressed in the words, "Only one, life of the worlds, King"[108]: "Only one" means that blessed G-d is utterly alone, in the *yichuda ila'ah* of *Atzilut*, where He and His radiance are truly one.[109]

6. ELICITING DIVINE RADIANCE

[Yet at the same time] He is called "the life of the worlds," for His quality as King spreads out through *tzimtzum*[110] to be King over the

---

104. Liturgy, blessings of the Shema.

105. At a level beyond its capacity to descend below and give life to lower worlds.

106. *Likkutei Torah*, *Pekudei* 6b, makes reference to *Baal Haturim* on this verse in Deuteronomy, who explains: "The word *echad* is written with a large *daled* to indicate that one should [mentally] acknowledge G-d King over the heavens, earth and the four corners of the world; also, so that one should not confuse [the *daled*] with a *resh*. Similarly, there is a large *resh* in the word *acher* in the verse 'Do not bow to *another* god,' so as not to confuse [the *resh*] with a *daled*. Another meaning: The verse *Shema Yisrael* contain a large *ayin* and a large *daled*, which spell the word *ed*, witness, as the verse (Isaiah 43:12), "*I have foretold and brought salvation and informed you; there was no strange [god] in your midst—you are my witnesses,' says G-d, 'and I am G-d.*" In addition, G-d is a Witness for Israel, as the verse states, 'I will be a swift witness...says G-d' (Malachi 3:5)."

In Kabbalistic terms, the *daled*, whose numerical value is four, refers to *malchut*, for *malchut* receives certain influence from the four *sefirot* of *tiferet*, *netzach*, *hod* and *yesod*. The large *daled* alludes to the essence of the attribute of *malchut* of *Atzilut*, which is too sublime to be vested in *Beriah*, *Yetzirah* and *Asiyah*. In the essence of *malchut*, the four directions—north, south, east and west—are totally abnegated, for there is no spacial existence there (*Likkutei Torah*, *Vayikra* 30b and 31c).

107. "I will exalt You" implies that it is possible

שֶׁזֶּהוּ בְּחִינַת הַהִתְנַשְּׂאוּת שֶׁמִּצַּד עַצְמוֹ דַּוְקָא וְנִקְרָא מֶלֶךְ מְרוֹמָם לְבַדּוֹ שֶׁהוּא נִבְדָּל בְּעֶרֶךְ הַרְבֵּה מִמַּה שֶּׁנִּקְרָא מֶלֶךְ עַל עוֹלָמוֹת הַנִּבְרָאִים כַּיָּדוּעַ שֶׁזֶּהוּ מִדַּת מַלְכוּת דַּאֲצִילוּת בִּבְחִינַת אֲצִילוּת מַמָּשׁ (וְהוּא עִנְיַן ד׳ רַבָּתִי דְּאֶחָד).

וְאָמַר שֶׁיְּרוֹמֵם גַּם לֵאלֹקִים בְּחִינַת כֹּחַ הָאֱלֹקִי בָּעוֹלָמוֹת לְמַעְלָה לִהְיוֹת בִּבְחִינַת הַמֶּלֶךְ שֶׁנִּקְרָא מֶלֶךְ מְרוֹמָם לְבַדּוֹ כו׳ וְהוּא יִחוּד מְמַלֵּא כָּל עָלְמִין בְּסוֹבֵב כָּל עָלְמִין.

וְזֶהוּ עִנְיַן יָחִיד חֵי הָעוֹלָמִים מֶלֶךְ פֵּירוּשׁ יָחִיד, כְּמוֹ שֶׁהוּא לְבַדּוֹ יִתְבָּרֵךְ בְּיִחוּדָא עִלָּאָה דַּאֲצִילוּת דְּאִיהוּ וְחִיּוּהִי חַד מַמָּשׁ.

וְנִקְרָא חֵי הָעוֹלָמִים בְּהִתְפַּשְּׁטוּת דְּמִדַּת מֶלֶךְ לִהְיוֹת מֶלֶךְ לְעוֹלָם עַל יְדֵי צִמְצוּם כַּנַּ״ל וְזֶהוּ הָאוֹר הַנִּמְשָׁךְ

---

for the created being to exalt G-d. However, "the king who is exalted alone" implies that G-d is exalted far beyond man's capacity to exalt Him, i.e., a far more sublime level. So by reciting this verse King David sought to elevate *Elokim* to that sublime level of "self-exalted."

108. Liturgy, *Baruch She'amar*, Morning Service.

109. *Iggeret HaKodesh* ch. 20, pp. 258 and 260 quote from *Tikkunei Zohar*, Introduction, p. 3b: "He (*Iyhu*) and His vivifications (*chayohi*) are one; He and His causations (*garmohi*) are one—in them." Rabbi Shneur Zalman then explains: "His vivifications'—these are the lights (*orot*), and 'His causations'—these are the vessels (*kelim*)."

Both the world of *Atzilut*—etymologically connected with *etzel* ("near"), i.e. nearest to the Source of creation, the *Ein Sof*—and *yichuda ila'ah*, the unity of G-d within Himself as He is in His essence completely transcending all worlds, signify G-d's total oneness, expressed in the phrase quoted from *Baruch She'amar*.

110. TZIMTZUM. Self-contraction or self-limitation of the infinite *Or Ein Sof*, which allows finite worlds to exist. Prior to creation, there was only the infinite revelation of G-d—the *Or Ein Sof*—filling all existence. Within this infinite revelation, finite worlds and beings could not possibly exist. When it arose in G-d's Will to create the worlds and all their inhabitants, He contracted and concealed the *Or Ein Sof*, creating a "void" in which finite existence could endure.

world, and this is the radiance which spreads from above to below. (And this is like the large *daled* of *Echad*, and while saying it one bears in mind[111] to express G-d's kingship in the heavens and the earth and the four corners of the world.)[112]

And occasionally the liturgy reads: "the King who is the only one, life of the worlds,"[113] meaning that the King *who is exalted alone* is [actually] elicited to be *the life of the worlds.*

Similarly regarding the ascent[114] from below to above [that preceded the descent], exalting "my G-d, the king" as He is the king, the Only One, exalted alone—so that then G-d as He is in His essence should subsequently be elicited into the worlds. This is [the verse's conclusion], "and I will bless Your Name for ever and ever."

This is also the theme of *Blessed be the Name of the glory of His kingship for ever and ever* : *Malchut* is termed "Name," as in the verse "And David made a name,"[115] and we pray that the Name of the glory of His kingship should be blessed [i.e. elicited][116] below, also into the worlds of separation,[117] with the eternity of *Ein Sof.* The word *vaed* means "eternity,"[118] and is the equivalent of the word *Echad* (One) by exchanging letters.[119]

7. EXALTING G-D THROUGH OUR PRAISES

How can we exalt "my G-d, the King"? Through songs and praises,[120] in which one declares that all worlds and angels are absolutely ab-

---

111. Thus eliciting the radiance from its exalted sublime level.

112. *Berachot* 13b. This passage in the Talmud expresses the basic idea of what to think when saying the Shema: that G-d rules over the whole universe. In this *maamar*, the idea is explained in terms of the highest, most exalted level of the Divine, the transcendent level beyond existence, joining with the lower level of the Divine, which is actually the life-force and inner power of the universe. The moment of saying the Shema is a combination of the transcendent and immanent aspects of G-d. (See *Siddur Arizal, L'shem Yichud,* introduction to *Baruch She'amar.*)

113. Liturgy, *Yishtabach*, Morning Prayer.

114. Lit., "elevation," "raising."

115. II Samuel 8:13. In the *Zohar* (III:113a) this is interpreted in relation to the verse, "and David performed justice and *tzedakah* with all his people": "Rabbi Shimon wept and said: Who makes the Holy Name, every day? He who gives charity unto the poor…." (*Iggeret haKodesh*, section 5. See there)

116. *Bracha* has the connotation of *hamshacha*, flow, from the term in *Kilayim* 7:1 "*Hamavrich et hagefen*"—one who grafts a vine, by bending its top downwards back into the ground and bringing the top back out of the ground. This is done so that the vine can take new root, thus supplying more life-force to the vine from the ground.

מִלְּמַעְלָה לְמַטָּה (וּכְמוֹ בִּדְלֵי״ת רַבָּתִי שֶׁמְּכַוֵּין לְהַמְלִיכוֹ בַּשָּׁמַיִם וָאָרֶץ וְד׳ רוּחוֹת הָעוֹלָם).

וְכֵן לִפְעָמִים אוֹמְרִים מֶלֶךְ יָחִיד שֶׁנִּקְרָא מֶלֶךְ מְרוֹמָם לְבַדּוֹ נִמְשָׁךְ לִהְיוֹת חֵי הָעוֹלָמִים כו׳

וּכְמוֹ כֵן הוּא בִּבְחִינַת הָעֲלָאָה מִלְּמַטָּה לְמַעְלָה שֶׁיְּרוֹמֵם לֵאלֹקֵי הַמֶּלֶךְ כְּמוֹ שֶׁהוּא מֶלֶךְ יָחִיד מְרוֹמָם לְבַדּוֹ שֶׁיּוּמְשַׁךְ אַחַר כַּךְ כְּמוֹ שֶׁהוּא בְּעַצְמוּתוֹ גַּם בָּעוֹלָמוֹת וְזֶהוּ וַאֲבָרְכָה שִׁמְךָ לְעוֹלָם וָעֶד.

כְּמוֹ עִנְיַן בָּרוּךְ שֵׁם כְּבוֹד מַלְכוּתוֹ לְעוֹלָם וָעֶד כַּיָּדוּעַ שֶׁבְּחִינַת הַמַּלְכוּת נִקְרָא שֵׁם כְּמוֹ וַיַּעַשׂ דָּוִד שֵׁם וְיִתְבָּרֵךְ שֵׁם כְּבוֹד מַלְכוּתוֹ לְמַטָּה גַּם בָּעוֹלָמוֹת הַנִּפְרָדִים בִּבְחִינַת נִצְחִיּוּת דְּאֵין סוֹף וְזֶהוּ וָעֶד נִצְחִיּוּת בְּחִילּוּף אוֹתִיּוֹת דְּאֶחָד.

וּבַמֶּה יְרוֹמֵם לֵאלֹקֵי הַמֶּלֶךְ כו׳ הַיְינוּ עַל יְדֵי שִׁירוֹת וְתִשְׁבָּחוֹת שֶׁאוֹמֵר אֵיךְ שֶׁכָּל הָעוֹלָמוֹת וּמַלְאָכִים בְּטֵלִים

Baruch is in *malchut*, for *baruch* means *hamshacha*, as explained. This is related to *malchut* from the verse (I Kings 2:45) "*King Solomon shall be blessed,*" meaning, he received the blessing until he became *baruch*, "a blessed one." Moreover, *malchut* is the recipient of the flow from the six *midot* (*Likkutei Torah*, *Tazria* 22b).

117. *Olamot Hanifradim*, in Hebrew; our lower worlds where G-d is hidden and there is disunity.

118. *Eruvin* 54a.

119. See *Shaar Hayichud v'HaEmunah* ch. 7, 81b. Thus the eternity of *Ein Sof* flows down into the lower worlds.

CHILUF OTIYOT: According to the rules of Hebrew grammer, the letters in the *alef-bet* are divided into various groups, according to their source in the organs of speech, and the letters in each group are interchangeable. The letters *alef*, *hey*, *vav* and *yud* fall into one group. Therefore *alef* may be interchanged with *vav*. The letters *alef*, *chet*, *hey* and *ayin* fall into another category, thus, *chet* may be interchanged with *ayin*. Hence *echad* becomes *vaed*.

120. This places the *Ashrei* prayer in its context of *Pesukei d'Zimra,* Verses of Praise, in the Morning Service. By one's own song, and by mentioning the song of the angels, one elevates the G-dliness within the worlds so that it connects with the highest level, the Only One, and even *malchut* of *Ein Sof* itself, His Great Name, causing the Divine radiance and life-force to flow into the lower worlds.

negated, dissolving to nothing, through their song. Through this one elevates the quality of *malchut* in order that it should receive influx from *keter malchut*. The words *Keter yitnu lecha* ("they give a Crown to You") [in the *Kedushah* of *Musaf*] express this, as is known.

(EXPLANATION OF BARUCH SHE'AMAR)

(This is also the meaning of the words: "praised and extolled by His pious ones and servants"[121]—meaning souls and angels of the worlds *Beriah, Yetzirah, Asiyah*[122]—"and with the songs of David Your servant we will praise You..." and so on, until "and we will make You King... our King, our G-d" so that You should be "the Only One, life of the worlds, King"—below, as You are above—"praised and extolled for ever," with the eternity of *Ein Sof*, meaning *malchut* of *Ein Sof* itself, which is called "His great Name," as is known.)

8. G-D'S KINGSHIP IS EXPRESSED IN WORLDS WITHOUT END

Thus we say [in *Ashrei*] "To tell people"—meaning, the souls—"of His might": This "might" refers to the tremendous power of *tzimtzum*[123] in order that the glory of the Essence of His Kingship[124] should be expressed in worlds without limit, extending lower and lower, just as there is no limit above, in His exaltedness, in His very essence.

A proof [that the source of the worlds is the exalted Divine Essence[125]] is the fact that this Essence spreads also within the veiled Divine force, to become the source of the coming into being of worlds with infinite variety of detail.[126] Hence the verse, "Great is our Master, and [of] immense power"[127]—without any limit.

---

121. Liturgy, *Baruch she'amar*, the beginning of *Pesukei d'Zimra*.

122. THE FOUR WORLDS: Kabbalah and Chasidut explain the phenomenon of the creation of a finite physical universe by an Infinite Creator with the concept of *tzimtzum*, contraction and concealment. G-d effected a series of concealments of His presence and infinitude, resulting ultimately, in the creation of our physical universe, through a virtually total concealment of G-d. The non-corporeal intermediate steps between the Creator and this material world are called "Worlds," referring to the basic levels of spiritual existence in the creative process. The differentiation reflects their level of concealment of the Divine Light, the higher worlds receiving in a more revealed form.

In general, there are Four Worlds: *Atzilut* (World of Emanation—a state of proximity and relative unity with G-d); *Beriah* (World of Creation); *Yetzirah* (World of Formation); *Asiyah* (World of Action or Making—the final stage in the creative process). The four worlds have been compared to the elements inherent to building a house. Four stages are necessary: 1) A general idea, as yet undefined; 2) A definite idea of the house in one's mind; 3) The architectural plan or design; 4) The

מִמְּצִיאוּתָם לְגַמְרֵי מִיֵּשׁ לְאַיִן עַל יְדֵי שִׁיר וְרִינָּה כו׳ שֶׁעַל יְדֵי זֶה מַעֲלִים לִבְחִינַת הַמַּלְכוּת לְמַעְלָה לְקַבֵּל מִבְּחִינַת כֶּתֶר מַלְכוּת וְזֶהוּ כֶּתֶר יִתְּנוּ לְךָ כו׳ כַּיָּדוּעַ.

(וְזֶהוּ מְשׁוּבָּח וּמְפוֹאָר בִּלְשׁוֹן חֲסִידָיו וַעֲבָדָיו נְשָׁמוֹת וּמַלְאָכִים דִּבְרִיאָה־יְצִירָה־עֲשִׂיָּה וּבְשִׁירֵי דָּוִד עַבְדֶּךָ נְהַלֶּלְךָ כו׳ עַד וְנַמְלִיכְךָ מַלְכֵּינוּ אֱלֹקֵינוּ לִהְיוֹת יָחִיד חֵי הָעוֹלָמִים מֶלֶךְ גַּם לְמַטָּה כְּמוֹ לְמַעְלָה לִהְיוֹת מְשׁוּבָּח וּמְפוֹאָר עֲדֵי עַד בִּבְחִינַת נִצְחִיּוּת דְּאֵין סוֹף שֶׁהוּא מַלְכוּת דְּאֵין סוֹף עַצְמוֹ שֶׁנִּקְרָא שְׁמוֹ הַגָּדוֹל כַּיָּדוּעַ).

וְזֶהוּ לְהוֹדִיעַ לִבְנֵי אָדָם שֶׁהֵן הַנְּשָׁמוֹת גְּבוּרוֹתָיו בְּחִינַת רִיבּוּי הַכֹּחַ שֶׁל הַצִּמְצוּמִים כְּדֵי לִהְיוֹת הֲדַר כְּבוֹד מַלְכוּתוֹ הָעַצְמִיּוּת בָּעוֹלָמוֹת לְאֵין שִׁיעוּר לְמַטָּה כְּמוֹ שֶׁאֵין שִׁיעוּר לְמַעְלָה בְּהִתְנַשְּׂאוּת שֶׁמִּצַּד עַצְמוֹ מַמָּשׁ כו׳.

וּרְאָיָה לָזֶה הוּא מַה שֶּׁמִּתְפַּשֵּׁט גַּם בַּכֹּחַ הָאֱלֹקִי הַמְצוּמְצָם לִהְיוֹת מָקוֹר לְהִתְהַוּוּת הָעוֹלָמוֹת גַּם כֵּן בִּבְחִינַת הִתְחַלְּקוּת לְאֵין שִׁיעוּר כְּלָל וּכְלָל וּכְמוֹ שֶׁכָּתוּב גָּדוֹל אֲדוֹנֵינוּ וְרַב כֹּחַ לְאֵין שִׁיעוּר.

---

actual building of the house (*Tanya*, Bilingual Edition, Kehot 1998, p. 343 fn. 3; p. 844).

"Higher" (or "Supernal") and "Lower" refer to stages closer or more distant from the Creator, with a greater or lesser awareness of Him (not, of course, implying physical distance). Lower Worlds appear to be independent entities from the Creator.

Through the performance of *mitzvot* and subordination of the physical world to the Divine purpose, all Worlds are elevated, and experience a clearer apprehension of G-d. See *Mystical Concepts in Chassidism*, ch. 2 (Tzimtzum) and ch. 4 (Worlds).

123. *Tzimtzum* (see fn. 110), comes from *gevurah*, might and severity.

124. This phrase relates both to the continuation of the verse in *Ashrei*, and also to the second line of the Shema.

125. Rather than just a lower level of the *sefirot.*

126. The facts that the world is created and exists, and its infinite variety, express the source of all creation.

127. Psalm 147:5. This is also part of the *Pesukei d'Zimra.* See above, beg. chapter 4 and fn. 85.

9. THE INFINITE QUALITY OF EXISTENCE

(It is written in *Sefer Yetzirah*[128]: "the measure of the Creator of Existence[129] is 236 myriads of thousands of parsangs,"[130] and 236 is the numerical value[131] of *v'rav koach* ("immense power"), as explained elsewhere). It is also written, "maidens (*alamot*) without number"[132]—"Do not read the word as *alamot,* maidens, but as *olamot,* worlds."[133] [And another example of the myriad variety and number of G-d's creations is] the verse, "is there any number to His hosts?"[134]

(Now although the verse says "He brings out their hosts [i.e. the stars] by number"[135] [implying that there is a limit in existence], such is His might that He is able to veil His power [so that it is expressed in a finite number of stars]. Nonetheless, there is no limit to this spreading forth [of Divine creative power], as stated in *Sefer Yetzirah,* "five stones build 120 houses"[136]—like the 120 combinations of the five Hebrew letters of the Name Elokim—"from there on try and calculate, there is no limit!",[137] as explained elsewhere).

10. CONCLUSION OF THE EXPLANATION OF ASHREI

This is what is meant [in *Ashrei*] by the verse, "to tell people of His Might," and the next verse, "Your Kingship is the Kingship of all the worlds."[138]

---

128. *Sefer Yetzirah* (lit. Book of Creation): One of the oldest written sources of Kabbalah, it is attributed to the Patriarch Abraham. It has been the subject of over one hundred commentaries since it was first published in Mantua, 1562.

Chasidic teachings often quote this passage about *Shiur Komah* in the name of *Sefer Yetzirah.* Possibly the title *Sefer Yetzirah* is used to depict a genre of early Kabbalistic text, rather than a specific book.

129. SHIUR KOMAH: G-d, the only One who is *Ein Sof,* is endless and limitless and cannot be defined in the realms of time or space, above or below. This seemingly causes a difficulty for physical man, who is limited, to become united with G-d. Moreover, we find that regarding spirituality in terms of the Worlds and *sefirot,* etc., the expressions of "above" and "below" are indeed used to define space. To explain: There must obviously be certain limits as to how much the *keilim* (vessels) limit the *orot* (lights) from being over-exposed, in accordance with the conformed order of all the Worlds and *sefirot,* known as *Seder Hishtalshelut.* Thus, the *orot* and *keilim* of *Atzilut* and lower are given specific spiritual "sizes" by which they are emanated and measured. These sizes are more commonly known as the ten *sefirot,* which can be found in the physical man too. By way of these corresponding ten powers, man can become united with G-d. Collectively, the ten *sefirot* form a celestial "stature," similar to man—a terrestrial stature fashioned of the ten powers of the human soul (*chesed, gevurah,* etc.).

130. This is understood by the Kabbalists as an infinite number.

131. Each letter of the Hebrew alphabet has a

(וּכְמוֹ שֶׁכָּתוּב בְּסֵפֶר יְצִירָה דְּשִׁיעוּר קוֹמָה שֶׁל יוֹצֵר בְּרֵאשִׁית רל״ו רִבְבוֹת אֲלָפִים פַּרְסָאוֹת כו׳ בְּגִימַטְרִיָּא דְּוְרַב כֹּחַ כְּמוֹ שֶׁכָּתוּב בֵּיאוּרוֹ בְּמָקוֹם אַחֵר) וּכְמוֹ שֶׁכָּתוּב וַעֲלָמוֹת אֵין מִסְפָּר אַל תִּקְרֵי עֲלָמוֹת אֶלָּא עוֹלָמוֹת וּכְתִיב הֲיֵשׁ מִסְפָּר לִגְדוּדָיו כו׳.

(וְאַף עַל פִּי שֶׁנֶּאֱמַר הַמּוֹצִיא בְמִסְפָּר צְבָאָם הֵן הֵן גְּבוּרוֹתָיו לְצַמְצֵם כו׳ וְעִם כָּל זֶה אֵין שִׁיעוּר לְהִתְפַּשְּׁטוּת זו כְּמוֹ שֶׁכָּתוּב בְּסֵפֶר יְצִירָה ה׳ אֲבָנִים בּוֹנוֹת ק״ך בָּתִּים כְּמוֹ ק״ך צֵירוּפִים דְּשֵׁם אֱלֹקִים מִכָּאן וְאֵילָךְ צֵא וַחֲשׁוֹב עַד אֵין שִׁיעוּר כו׳ וּכְמוֹ שֶׁכָּתוּב בֵּיאוּר זֶה בְּמָקוֹם אַחֵר).

וְזֶהוּ לְהוֹדִיעַ לִבְנֵי אָדָם גְּבוּרוֹתָיו וְאַחַר כַּךְ אָמַר מַלְכוּתְךָ מַלְכוּת כָּל עוֹלָמִים וְדַי לַמֵּבִין.

---

numeric value. The first nine letters, from *alef* through *tet*, equal one through nine respectively. The next nine letters, *yud* through *tzadik*, equal ten through ninety respectively. The next four letters, *kuf* through *tav*, equal one hundred through four hundred respectively.

(The intermediary numbers are created by combining single Hebrew characters of different value. For example, two hundred and thirty-six would be *resh lamed vav* – רלו. Five hundred is represented by *tav kuf* – תק. *Tav reish* equals 600, *tav tav kuf* – תתק equals 900, etc. One thousand is represented by a single letter followed by an apostrophe. For example, 1001 would be written: *alef ' alef* – א'א.)

132. Song of Songs 6:8.

133. Introduction to *Tikkunei Zohar*, 14b. Frequently quoted in Chassidic teachings.

134. Job 25:3. Discussed in Talmud, *Chagigah* 13b. See *Tanya*, ch. 46, 65b.

135. Isaiah 40:26.

136. 4:12. One can make 120 combinations of 5 letters (5 factorial: 5x4x3x2).

137. Ibid. With more and more letters of the Hebrew alphabet coming into play, the number of possible combinations grows larger and larger, creating the myriad worlds with all their individual features. The purpose of this paragraph is to demonstrate that there are both finite numbers and infinite variety in Creation. See *Chagigah* ibid.

138. Which expresses the theme of this explanation of *Ashrei*.

(Hence the *Zohar's* comment on the verse, "G-d, do not be silent"[139]: "the Lower Radiance calls continuously to the Higher Radiance, and is never at rest."[140] This complies with the verse "in order that glory should sing to You"[141]: the lower glory of *malchut* in the lower worlds of *B'ya*[142] sings to the upper glory of *keter malchut*, as explained above).

---

139. Psalms 83:2.

140. See the end of chapter 3 above. The Lower Radiance is *memale kol almin*, which calls to and connects with the Higher Radiance, *sovev kol almin*, and then flows down

(וְזֶהוּ מַה שֶּׁכָּתוּב בַּזֹּהַר עַל פָּסוּק אֱלֹקִים אַל דֳּמִי לָךְ דִּנְהוֹרָא תַּתָּאָה קָארֵי תָּדִיר לִנְהוֹרָא עִילָּאָה וְלָא שָׁכִיךְ לְעָלְמִין וְהוּא מַה שֶּׁכָּתוּב לְמַעַן יְזַמֶּרְךָ כָבוֹד הַתַּחְתּוֹן דְּמַלְכוּת בִּבְרִיאָה־יְצִירָה־עֲשִׂיָּה לְכָבוֹד עֶלְיוֹן דִּבְחִינַת כֶּתֶר מַלְכוּת כַּנַ״ל:)

again—this time, through all levels of existence.

141. Psalms 30:13.

142. Acronym for *Beriah*, *Yezirah*, *Asiyah*. See footnote 122.

SUMMARY
OF CHAPTER FOUR

The expression of the spiritual oil is achieved by *hitbonenut*, contemplation in prayer, of which there are two kinds: 1) *Memalei kol almin*, the Divine Name *Elokim—yichuda tata'ah*; 2) *Sovev kol almin*, the Divine Name *Havaya—yichuda ila'ah*.

Yichuda tata'ah: This method of contemplation is described via a commentary on *Pesukei d'Zimra* (Verses of Praise) in *Shacharit*, the commentary for the most part focuses on Psalm 145, *Ashrei*, as follows:

I will exalt You, my G-d [Elokei], *the King*:

Malchut of *Atzilut* consists of two aspects: a) power, mastery; b) judgement, sovereignty. *Malchut* is the last of the *sefirot* and the primary source for all *creatio ex nihilo*. It is rooted in *the King who is exalted alone*.

King David prayed that the G-dly active power—*Elokei*—be united with *the King who is exalted alone*, by way of *yichuda tata'ah* of *memalei kol almin*. Hence, *Only One, life of the worlds*: Just as the level of G-dly exaltedness is united by way of *yichuda ila'ah* with the ten *sefirot* of *Atzilut*, similarly may *malchut* be elevated (I will *exalt* You) to subsequently elicit—

. . . *and I will bless Your Name forever*:

I.e., *I will elicit*, through my Divine service, *Your* essential *Name*—the source of *malchut*, that it may flow *forever*—with the infinity of *Ein Sof*.

This elevation takes place through *song and praise by the tongue of His pious ones* (the souls) *and His servants* (the angels). This is *To make known to men* (the souls) *His mighty acts*, the infinite division within Creation, which comes from the essential transcendence of *keter malchut*. Thus, it is specifically *malchut* that infuses life-force into the infinite number of creations, and yet to each in a set, distinctive measure. The worshipper is the agent for this cosmic spiritual interaction.

By contemplating the above, the worshipper reveals the spiritual oil described in chapter 3.

INTRODUCTION TO CHAPTER FIVE

The hoped-for effect of the system of contemplation, described in the previous chapter, is inner transformation of the Animal Soul and one's natural passions. The passions then become focused on love of G-d instead of their natural material concerns. This is the effect of the dark flame, consuming and transforming the wick.

This is paralleled by a similar process taking place in the spiritual realms. Just as the Animal Soul is abnegated before the Divine, so are the seventy heavenly princes (which are the source of the seventy nations of the world) abnegated before G-d. This has a messianic significance, triggered, it would seem, through the person's contemplation during prayer.

There is, however, a higher form of contemplation, corresponding to the bright flame. Instead of focusing on *memalei kol almin*, the worshipper aims higher and higher, focusing on *sovev kol almin* and then higher still, to ever higher levels, with simple self-surrender before the Essence of the Divine.

5.
MORE ON CONTEMPLATION

INNER TRANSFORMATION

When one contemplates with the depths of mind and heart on *yichuda tata'ah* of *malchut* within the worlds—*memale kol almin*—the power of the Divine radiance which gives existence to all worlds from the void, as explained above (concerning *Baruch shem k'vod malchuto l'olam vaed*),[143] then one will become inspired in his heart with a Divine love, loving G-d with all his heart—with both inclinations, as the verse states "and you should love G-d with all your heart"[144] [and the Sages comment: you should love G-d with both inclinations, with your Good inclination and your Evil inclination[145]].

This is because through the G-dly understanding [of *yichuda tata'ah*] which is absorbed properly in one's mind and heart, one's natural heart of flesh will also become excited. It will feel a longing and a wonderful yearning with flames of spiritual fire until he loathes [his present state] and will transform every foreign or negative desire coming from his natural passions,[146] to have only "one heart," focused on his Father in Heaven, just as the soul itself yearns with Divine longing—a yearning which is the very opposite of the natural desire of the physical body, which is called "the spirit of the animal descending below."[147]

He will experience a genuine enthusiasm, from the inner depths of his heart, affecting all the aspects of his natural soul. This form of contemplation, focusing on the Divine energy which is in the worlds, is very close to a person. Hence he can perceive it even with his physical eyes, as it says, "raise your eyes to the heights and see Who created these."[148] The term "see" implies as with real physical sight, to the extent that one can completely transform one's foreign desires into a fiery enthusiasm of longing for G-d alone. Thus, even one's natural passion, which is full of evil, is transformed into true Divine holiness.

---

143. See chapter 4 above, #6 of the explanation of *Ashrei*.

144. Deuteronomy 6:5.

145. *Mishnah, Berachot* 9:5.

146. Literally, "heat."

(ה)

וְהִנֵּה כַּאֲשֶׁר הָאָדָם יִתְבּוֹנֵן בְּעוֹמֶק דַּעְתּוֹ וְלִבּוֹ בִּבְחִינַת יִחוּדָא תַּתָּאָה דְּמַלְכוּת בָּעוֹלָמוֹת בְּחִינַת מְמַלֵּא כָּל עָלְמִין שֶׁהוּא בְּכֹחַ הָאוֹר הָאֱלֹקִי הַמְהַוֶּוה כָּל הָעוֹלָמוֹת מֵאַיִן לְיֵשׁ כַּנַ״ל (בְּבָרוּךְ שֵׁם כְּבוֹד מַלְכוּתוֹ לְעוֹלָם וָעֶד) יִתְפָּעֵל בְּלִבּוֹ בְּאַהֲבָה אֱלֹקִית לֶאֱהוֹב אֶת ה׳ בְּכָל לְבָבוֹ וְהַיְינוּ בִּשְׁנֵי יְצָרֶיךָ כְּמוֹ שֶׁכָּתוּב וְאָהַבְתָּ בְּכָל לְבָבְךָ.

וְהוּא שֶׁעַל יְדֵי הַשָּׂגָה אֱלֹקִית הַזֹּאת הַנִּקְלֶטֶת הֵיטֵב בְּמוֹחַ וְלֵב יִתְפָּעֵל גַּם בְּלֵב בָּשָׂר הַטִּבְעִי לִהְיוֹת בּוֹ כִּלָּיוֹן וּתְשׁוּקָה נִפְלָאָה בְּרִשְׁפֵּי אֵשׁ שַׁלְהֶבֶת יָ־הּ עַד שֶׁיִּמָּאֵס וְיֵהָפֵךְ כָּל רָצוֹן זָר וְרַע דְּחוֹם הַטִּבְעִי לִהְיוֹת לוֹ רַק לֵב אֶחָד לְאָבִיו שֶׁבַּשָּׁמַיִם כו׳ כְּמוֹ שֶׁהַנְּשָׁמָה בְּעַצְמָהּ תִּכְסוֹף בִּתְשׁוּקָה הָאֱלֹקִית הֵיפֶךְ טֶבַע הַגּוּף הַחוּמְרִי שֶׁנִּקְרָא רוּחַ הַבְּהֵמָה שֶׁיּוֹרֶדֶת לְמַטָּה כו׳.

בְּהִתְפַּעֲלוּת אֲמִתִּית מִקֶּרֶב וְלֵב עָמוֹק בְּכָל כּוֹחוֹת הַנֶּפֶשׁ הַטִּבְעִית כו׳ לְפִי שֶׁהִתְבּוֹנְנוּת זֹאת דְּכֹחַ הָאֱלֹקִי בָּעוֹלָמוֹת קְרוֹבָה לְנֶפֶשׁ הָאָדָם לִרְאוֹת גַּם בְּעֵינֵי בָשָׂר כְּמוֹ שֶׁנֶּאֱמַר שְׂאוּ מָרוֹם עֵינֵיכֶם וּרְאוּ מִי בָרָא אֵלֶּה פֵּירוּשׁ וּרְאוּ כְּמוֹ בִּרְאִיָּה חוּשִׁיּוּת מַמָּשׁ כו׳ עַד שֶׁיָּכוֹל לִהְיוֹת הִתְהַפְּכוּת הָרְצוֹנוֹת זָרוֹת לְגַמְרֵי דְּהַיְינוּ לִהְיוֹת מִתְהַפְּכִים בְּהִתְפַּעֲלוּת רִשְׁפֵּי אֵשׁ הַתְּשׁוּקָה לַה׳ לְבַדּוֹ וְנִמְצָא גַּם הַחוּם הַטִּבְעִי שֶׁמָּלֵא רָע נֶהְפָּךְ לִקְדוּשָּׁה הָאֱלֹקִית מַמָּשׁ.

---

147. Ecclesiastes 3:21. Just as his soul naturally yearns only for G-d, his animal passions will also be filled with spiritual longing, due to his contemplation of *yichuda tata'ah*.

148. Isaiah 40:26.

(The person is then called "pure of heart, who does not turn his soul to worthless things,"[149] nor his desires at all, focusing only on G-d alone, as expressed in the words "who is there for me in Heaven, and I want none other than You in the world, my flesh and my heart long for You.[150])

Eventually his heart will become completely pure, at least at that moment, with absolutely genuine surrender of his self to the Divine *Ayin*. (For the Divine radiance of *malchut* of the worlds rests on him. When this shines on high, over the supernal angels, they are totally abnegated. [Therefore his own animal soul is also abnegated.[151]])

THE DARK RADIANCE

This is just like the image of the wick that burns with the flame with which it is kindled, transforming it to the essence of fire and light. Similarly, the body, comprising the fire and natural heat of evil desires, is transformed into longing for the Divine, which is termed the fire of the sacred flame[152] of the Divine Soul, dedicated solely to G-d. Thus, the verse states, "[you should love G-d] with all your heart,"[153] [i.e.] "with both your inclinations," so that also the evil inclination in the left side of the heart[154] should love G-d with the excitement of the fire of the sacred flame of the Divine.

Thus, there can be genuine Divine enthusiasm in the heart of flesh, as in the verse, "my heart and my flesh sing."[155] However this does not last a long time, for the oil of the quality of selflessness, described above, does not flow into the wick.

---

149. Psalms 24:4.

150. Psalms 73:25-6. The verse is explained in this spirit in *Hayom Yom*, 18 Kislev, quoting Rabbi Menachem Mendel, the *Tzemach Tzedek*: The love expressed in "Beside You I wish for nothing," means that one should desire nothing other than G-d, not even "heaven" or "earth," i.e. Higher *Gan Eden* and Lower *Gan Eden*, for these were created with a mere *yud* (the first and smallest letter of G-d's name *Havaya*).... The Love is to be directed to Him alone, to His very Being and Essence. This was actually expressed by my master and teacher (Rabbi Schneur Zalman of Liadi) when he as in a state of *d'veikut* (ecstatic, cleaving devotion to G-d) and he exclaimed as follows: *I want nothing at all! I don't want your gan eden, I don't want your olam haba... I want nothing but You alone.*

151. Every physical creation must have a celestial source, from which it receives its life-force and existence. Its very being and physical characteristics resemble their spiritual source, albeit physically. All living creatures are derived from the spiritual angels that are found in the Divine Chariot and consequently, the faces of the lion and the ox in the

(וְנִקְרָא בַּר לֵבָב מַמָּשׁ אֲשֶׁר לֹא נָשָׂא לַשָּׁוְא נַפְשׁוֹ וּרְצוֹנוֹ כְּלָל רַק לַה׳ לְבַדּוֹ כְּמוֹ מִי לִי בַשָּׁמָיִם וְעִמְּךָ לֹא חָפַצְתִּי בָאָרֶץ כָּלָה שְׁאֵרִי וּלְבָבִי כו׳).

עַד שֶׁנַּעֲשֶׂה לִבּוֹ לֵב טָהוֹר לְגַמְרֵי בְּאוֹתָהּ שָׁעָה עַל כָּל פָּנִים בִּבְחִינַת בִּיטּוּל הַיֵּשׁ לָאַיִן הָאֱלֹקִי בֶּאֱמֶת לַאֲמִתּוֹ (מִפְּנֵי שֶׁשּׁוֹרֶה עָלָיו בְּחִינַת אוֹר הָאֱלֹקִי דְּמַלְכוּת בָּעוֹלָמוֹת כְּמוֹ שֶׁמֵּאִיר לְמַעְלָה בְּמַלְאָכִים עֶלְיוֹנִים כְּשֶׁבְּטֵלִים בִּמְצִיאוּת כו׳).

וְזֶהוּ מַמָּשׁ כְּדִמְיוֹן הַפְּתִילָה שֶׁדּוֹלֶקֶת בְּשַׁלְהֶבֶת אֵשׁ הַנִּדְלָק בָּהּ שֶׁנֶּהְפֶּכֶת לְמַהוּת אֵשׁ וְאוֹר כו׳ כַּךְ נֶהְפָּךְ הַגּוּף שֶׁהוּא אֵשׁ וְחוּם הַטִּבְעִי שֶׁל תַּאֲוָה רָעָה עַצְמָהּ לְמַהוּת הַתְּשׁוּקָה הָאֱלֹקִית שֶׁנִּקְרָא רִשְׁפֵּי אֵשׁ שַׁלְהֶבֶת יָ־הּ דִּנְשָׁמָה הָאֱלֹקִית כַּנַּ״ל לִהְיוֹת רַק לַה׳ לְבַדּוֹ כְּמוֹ שֶׁכָּתוּב בְּכָל לְבָבְךָ בִּשְׁנֵי יְצָרֶיךָ שֶׁגַּם הַיֵּצֶר הָרָע שֶׁבֶּחָלָל הַשְּׂמָאלִי יֶאֱהוֹב אֶת ה׳ בְּהִתְפַּעֲלוּת רִשְׁפֵּי אֵשׁ שַׁלְהֶבֶת יָ־הּ הָאֱלֹקִי מַמָּשׁ.

וּכְמוֹ שֶׁאָנוּ רוֹאִים שֶׁיֵּשׁ הִתְפַּעֲלוּת אֱלֹקוּת מַמָּשׁ בְּלֵב בָּשָׂר דַּוְקָא וּכְמוֹ לִבִּי וּבְשָׂרִי יְרַנְּנוּ כו׳ רַק שֶׁאֵינוֹ נִמְשָׁךְ זְמַן רַב מִטַּעַם שֶׁאֵין בְּחִינַת הַשֶּׁמֶן דְּכֹחַ מָ״ה הַנַּ״ל נִמְשָׁךְ אַחַר הַפְּתִילָה כַּנַּ״ל.

Divine Chariot are the sources for all physical animals and beasts.

The animal soul is rooted not in the *Sefirot* but in the chariot. It then descends to a lowly derivative (dregs) of the *ofanim*, which are of a lower order than the *chayot*. The animal soul is derived from the "dregs" of the *ofanim*, but is originally rooted in the face of the ox of the Divine chariot (*Likkutei Torah*, *Vayikra* 2b). See footnote 281 at length.

152. Lit., "flame of Y-H"—G-d.

153. The Hebrew word *lev* is translated as "heart." Here, the verse uses the term *levavcha*, from which the Sages imply (the plural, i.e.,) the necessity to serve G-d with "*two* hearts," i.e., the good inclination *and* the evil inclination. Chasidut discusses at length how one may serve G-d with the evil inclination, primarily by not carrying out one's evil desires, and also to the extent of channeling the energy and excitement with which one was to practice a negative act, making use of that energy for performing positive actions.

154. See *Tanya*, ch. 9, p. 14a.

155. Psalms 84:3.

It was explained above that this [enthusiasm] is termed the "dark radiance," the black fire which gradually burns and consumes the wick. Similarly, the Divine radiance of the ecstasy of the soul—on account of its awareness of *memale kol almin*—burns and consumes one's natural desires,[156] to transform them to the radiance of holiness.

THE PARALLEL IN SPIRITUAL REALMS

(This parallels in the spiritual realms, when *malchut* of *Atzilut* is vested in the worlds, it is like the soul being vested in the body, and *malchut* is called "the soul of all that lives"[157]—*memale kol almin*, and is also called the "dark radiance." For it has a transforming effect, causing the abnegation of existence before the Divine in all the worlds, including also the seventy patron-angels of *nogah*[158] of *Asiyah*. They too become abnegated and absorbed in the Living G-d through song.[159]

[This idea is expressed] as the verses "G-d reigns over the nations"[160] and "Praise the L-rd all you nations,"[161] and also "render to the L-rd, O families of nations."[162] There are many similar verses in Scripture, like "let all the earth fear the L-rd,"[163] "let all the earth sing in jubilation to the L-rd."[164] This [transformation of the spiritual realms so that they recognize G-d's Kingship] is just like the transformation of the seven evil emotions of the natural soul in a human being.)[165]

---

156. Lit., "heart."

157. Liturgy, Shabbat morning.

158. SEVENTY PATRON-ANGELS OF NOGAH: *Zohar* III:244a (in *Raya Mehemna*) and *Tikkunei Zohar* 24:69a, speak of the seventy nations, that their vivification is by way of an investment of the seventy extraneous patron-angels who are appointed over them. That is, a spark from the "word of G-d" called *malchut* of *Asiyah*, descends and radiates over the supernal patron-angels, encompassing them from aloft, but does not truly vest itself in them. Rather, the energy issues to them from this radiation shining over them from aloft, in a mode of encompassment. The energy issues to the heathens, cattle, beasts, and fowl that are in their lands, and to the physical heaven and earth, i.e., the planets. The heavens and the earth, the cattle, beasts and fowl that are pure, are influenced by *kelipat nogah* (see fn. 35), while the impure animals and the souls of the heathens are influenced by the other *kelipot*.

The creations that receive influence from the seventy patron-angels of *nogah* are esteemed as truly nothing in relation to the pa-

וּמְבוֹאָר לְמַעְלָה שֶׁזֶּהוּ הַנִּקְרָא נְהוֹרָא אוּכָּמָא אֵשׁ הַשָּׁחוֹר הַשּׂוֹרֵף וּמְכַלֶּה לַפְּתִילָה מְעַט מְעַט כו׳ כַּךְ אוֹר הָאֱלֹקִי שֶׁבְּהִתְפַּעֲלוּת הַנְּשָׁמָה מֵהַשָּׂגָה דִּמְמַלֵּא כָּל עָלְמִין הַנַּ״ל שׂוֹרֵף וּמְכַלֶּה לַלֵּב הַטִּבְעִי לְהַפְּכוֹ לְאוֹר הַקְּדוּשָּׁה.

(וּכְמוֹ כֵן לְמַעְלָה בְּמַלְכוּת דַּאֲצִילוּת בְּהִתְלַבְּשׁוּתָהּ בָּעוֹלָמוֹת שֶׁזֶּהוּ גַּם כֵּן כְּמוֹ הִתְלַבְּשׁוּת הַנְּשָׁמָה בַּגּוּף וְנִקְרָא נִשְׁמַת כָּל חַי כו׳ שֶׁנִּקְרָא מְמַלֵּא כָּל עָלְמִין נִקְרָא גַּם כֵּן נְהוֹרָא אוּכָּמָא כַּנַּ״ל לְפִי שֶׁמְּהַפֵּךְ לִהְיוֹת בִּיטּוּל הַיֵּשׁ לְאַיִן בְּכָל הָעוֹלָמוֹת עַד גַּם הָע׳ שָׂרִים דְּנוֹגַהּ דַּעֲשִׂיָּה שֶׁגַּם הֵם בְּטֵלִים וְנִכְלָלִים בֵּאלֹקִים חַיִּים בְּשִׁירָה.

כְּמוֹ שֶׁכָּתוּב מָלַךְ אֱלֹקִים עַל גּוֹיִם וּכְתִיב הַלְלוּ אֶת ה׳ כָּל גּוֹיִם כו׳ וְכֵן הָבוּ לַה׳ מִשְׁפְּחוֹת עַמִּים כו׳ וּכְהַאי גַּוְונָא רַבּוֹת בִּכְתוּבִים כְּמוֹ יִרְאוּ מֵה׳ כָּל הָאָרֶץ כו׳ הָרִיעוּ לַה׳ כָּל הָאָרֶץ כו׳ וְזֶהוּ כְּמוֹ הִתְהַפְּכוּת ז׳ מִדּוֹת רָעוֹת דְּנֶפֶשׁ הַטִּבְעִית מַמָּשׁ בָּאָדָם הַתַּחְתּוֹן כַּיָּדוּעַ).

---

tron-angels. Moreover, the seventy patron-angels of *nogah* themselves are esteemed as truly nothing in relation to the vivification issuing to them from the aforementioned "word of G-d" which radiates over them. (*Iggeret HaKodesh*, ch. 25)

159. So when *malchut* of *Atzilut* is vested within the worlds, all the worlds, including their vivification—the seventy patron-angels—are abnegated and absorbed in G-dliness through song, with no entity of their own.

160. Psalms 47:9.

161. Ibid. 117:1.

162. Ibid. 96:7; I Chronicles 16:28.

163. Psalms 33:8.

164. Ibid. 100:1.

165. Note the chain of connection: the seven emotions relate to the seven nations of Canaan, and in turn to the seventy nations of the world. Thus an individual's inner conquest of his or her own emotions is parallel to (or initiates) the positive transformation of humanity and of the universe.

WICKED AND RIGHTEOUS

(The verse "the lamp of the wicked sputters"[166] means that even when they are "beaten" [by the problems of life] their lamp sputters and flickers even more, for they are totally separated [from holiness] by being involved with complete evil from the realm of the three totally impure *kelipot*. However, regarding *tzaddikim* the verse states, "the light of the righteous [rejoices],"[167] and "a body in which the radiance of the soul does not shine, should be 'beaten' and then the light shines, like a log in which the flame does not catch."[168] Thus it is evident by experiencing difficulties[169] regarding children, health and livelihood, the light of the soul shines within him, prompting him to thoughts of *teshuvah* with a contrite heart, truly submitting to G-d and feeling intense emotions of love and fear of G-d within the longing of the fire of the sacred flames of the soul.

Therein lies the difference between *nogah* in which good and evil are combined, and the *three impure kelipot* of complete evil, as it is written, "and you will turn back and see the difference between the righteous and the wicked, between one who serves G-d and one who does not."[170] However, even in the case of the wicked, it is written, "they will be cleansed and purified,"[171] and as the verse, "those who are lost... will return,"[172] "for no one will be completely driven away."[173] Also, of the nations of the world the verse states, "then I will turn to the nations [a clear tongue]."[174])

THE BRIGHT FLAME: EVER HIGHER

Now, this discussion concerned the dark flame which burns at the wick. However, the bright flame described above, which is termed "the light which illuminates," is derived specifically from the second kind of contemplation, of *sovev kol almin*.

---

166. Proverbs 13:9.

167. Ibid.

168. See *Zohar* III:168a; *Tanya* ch. 29, p. 35b.

169. Lit., "beating."

170. Malachi 3:18. The explanation as to how the verse can imply that *nogah* would be compared to a *tzaddik*, (who serves G-d), while the three impure *kelipot* are compared to a *rasha*, (one who does not serve G-d at all) is thus: The verse does not discuss a "*tzaddik*" in its general connotation, rather one who has the potential to be a *tzaddik*, i.e., one that is a *tzaddik* in his inner self, but suffers from a *kelipah* which covers him (*nogah*). This individual would benefit from a "beating," for it would prompt him to *teshuvah*, thus de-

(וּמַה שֶׁכָּתוּב וְנֵר רְשָׁעִים יִדְעָךְ הַיְינוּ גַּם כְּשֶׁמְּבַטְּשִׁים אוֹתָם יִדְעָךְ וְיִקְפֹּץ נֵרָם יוֹתֵר כְּשֶׁהֵן בִּבְחִינַת פֵּירוּד גָּמוּר מִבְּחִינַת הָרָע גָּמוּר דְּג׳ קְלִיפּוֹת הַטְּמֵאוֹת לְגַמְרֵי כוּ׳ וּבַצַּדִּיקִים כְּתִיב וְאוֹר צַדִּיקִים כוּ׳ וְגוּפָא דְּלָא סָלִיק בֵּיהּ נְהוֹרָא דְּנִשְׁמְתָא מְבַטְּשִׁין לֵיהּ וְסָלִיק בֵּיהּ כוּ׳ כְּאָעָא דְּלָא סָלִיק בֵּיהּ נְהוֹרָא כוּ׳ וְכַנִּרְאֶה בְּחוּשׁ שֶׁעַל יְדֵי בִּיטּוּשׁ בְּבָנֵי חַיֵּי וּמְזוֹנֵי בַּגּוּף יָאִיר בּוֹ אוֹר הַנְּשָׁמָה לַעֲשׂוֹת בּוֹ הִרְהוּר תְּשׁוּבָה בְּלֵב נִשְׁבָּר מְאֹד וּלְהִכָּנַע בֶּאֱמֶת לַה׳ וּלְהִתְפָּעֵל בְּאַהֲבָה וְיִרְאָה בִּתְשׁוּקַת רִשְׁפֵּי אֵשׁ שַׁלְהֶבֶת יָ־הּ דְּנִשְׁמָה.

וּבָזֶה הוּא הַהֶפְרֵשׁ בֵּין נוֹגַהּ דִּמְעוֹרָב טוֹב וָרָע לְג׳ קְלִיפּוֹת הַטְּמֵאוֹת דְּרָע גָּמוּר וּכְמוֹ שֶׁנֶּאֱמַר וְשַׁבְתֶּם וּרְאִיתֶם בֵּין צַדִּיק לְרָשָׁע בֵּין עוֹבֵד אֱלֹקִים כוּ׳ אַךְ גַּם בָּרְשָׁעִים כְּתִיב וְיִתְלַבְּנוּ וְיִתְבָּרְרוּ כוּ׳ וּכְמוֹ שֶׁנֶּאֱמַר וּבָאוּ הָאוֹבְדִים כוּ׳ כִּי לֹא יִדַּח מִמֶּנּוּ נִדָּח וְגַם בְּאוּמּוֹת הָעוֹלָם כְּתִיב אָז אֶהְפּוֹךְ אֶל עַמִּים כוּ׳.)

וְהִנֵּה כָּל זֶה הוּא בְּחִינַת נְהוֹרָא אוּכָמָא שֶׁנִּדְלָק בַּפְּתִילָה כַּנַּ״ל אֲבָל בְּחִינַת נְהוֹרָא חִיוּוְרָא הַנַּ״ל שֶׁנִּקְרָא אוֹר הַמֵּאִיר הוּא בָּא מִבְּחִינַת הִתְבּוֹנְנוּת הַשְּׁנִיָּה דִּבְחִינַת סוֹבֵב כָּל עָלְמִין דַּוְקָא.

---

stroying that shell. A *rasha* is of a lower stature, for even a "beating" would accomplish nothing.

On the other hand, as the paragraph continues, the wicked are not totally doomed, for in the future "those who are lost… will return."

171. Cf. Daniel 12:10.

172. Isaiah 27:13.

173. Cf. II Samuel 14:14.

174. Zephaniah 3:9. All these verses refer to the future, when Moshiach will come. Apparently the author's intention here is that even the wicked, who parallel the three impure *kelipot*, will indeed return to G-d in the future.

This [contemplation] is on the name *Havaya* in *Atzilut*, in the *yichuda ila'ah* expressed in the [first verse of] Shema Yisrael. It is known that this relates to the ten *sefirot* of *Atzilut* which are one with the Essence of the Infinite, for He and His life-force are truly one,[175] as stated [in the Shema], "the L-rd is our G-d, the L-rd is One," truly one with the pure unity of the Infinite itself. This is far beyond the aspect of *malchut* that becomes the source of the worlds, as is written, "with You is the source of life."[176]

The Essence of the Infinite is also higher and beyond even the world of *Atzilut*, for it states, "You are one, beyond number,"[177] meaning beyond the number of the ten *sefirot*, because "before one, what do you count?"[178]

This transcendence is termed the "ten *sefirot* without qualities,"[179] meaning without any quality at all, for "they are beyond all these attributes."[180] This is the very essence of the Infinite, for also the way that He veils[181] Himself in order to be the source of the ten *sefirot* of *Atzilut* involves only a mere gleam—termed the *kav* and *chut* [of radiance][182] which extends from *malchut* of *Ein Sof* itself, through the initial *tzimtzum*,[183] as is known, just like [the veiling in between] *Atzilut* and the lower worlds of *Beriah*, *Yeztirah* and *Asiyah*.[184]

Concerning this, the verse states, "For with You is the source of..." all the life of the worlds of Atzilut, *Beriah*, *Yetzirah* and *Asiyah*. This [higher level] is what is termed "*sovev kol almin.*" It surrounds the four worlds of *Aztilut*, *Beriah*, *Yetzirah* and *Asiyah* equally. This is what is meant by "King, Only One, life of the *worlds*"[185] on a level

---

175. See footnote 109.

176. Psalms 36:10. The source of life, *malchut*, is secondary to and apparently separate from the Divine Essence. Hence it is termed "*with You*," implying separateness.

177. *Tikkunei Zohar*, Introduction, 17a.

178. *Sefer Yetzirah* 1:7, meaning, the Entity before (higher; preceding) the first of the *sefirot* is not countable.

179. Ibid. 1:2 (see commentaries there). *Bli mah bli mahut*, in Hebrew, which literally means, without self-awareness. Before the ten *sefirot* are actualized into *sefirot*, they exist within the Essence of *Or Ein Sof*. Regarding this stage *Sefer Yetzirah* describes the ten *sefirot* as "without 'what'" i.e., without any self-awareness or substance.

180. *Tikkunei Zohar* ibid.

181. Lit., "contracts"—see footnote 110.

182. KAV: Lit., line, also known as *chut*, thread.

וְהוּא בְּשֵׁם הוי״ה דַּאֲצִילוּת בְּיִחוּדָא עִלָּאָה דִּשְׁמַע יִשְׂרָאֵל כַּנַּ״ל וְכַיָּדוּעַ שֶׁזֶּהוּ בְּעֶשֶׂר סְפִירוֹת דַּאֲצִילוּת שֶׁמְּיוּחָדִים בְּעַצְמוּת אֵין סוֹף בָּרוּךְ הוּא דְּאִיהוּ וְחִיּוּהִי חַד מַמָּשׁ כְּמוֹ שֶׁכָּתוּב ה׳ אֱלֹקֵינוּ ה׳ אֶחָד מַמָּשׁ בַּאַחְדוּת פְּשׁוּטָה דְּאֵין סוֹף עַצְמוֹ שֶׁהוּא לְמַעְלָה מַעְלָה מִבְּחִינַת הַמַּלְכוּת שֶׁנַּעֲשָׂה מָקוֹר לָעוֹלָמוֹת וּכְמוֹ שֶׁכָּתוּב כִּי עִמְּךָ מְקוֹר חַיִּים כו׳ כַּיָּדוּעַ.

וְכַךְ הוּא לְמַעְלָה מַעְלָה גַּם מֵעוֹלָם הָאֲצִילוּת שֶׁהֲרֵי א׳ אַנְתְּ הוּא חַד וְלָא בְּחוּשְׁבָּן פֵּירוּשׁ לָא בְּחוּשְׁבַּן י׳ סְפִירוֹת דִּלְפְנֵי אֶחָד מָה אַתָּה סוֹפֵר.

וְנִקְרָאִים עֶשֶׂר סְפִירוֹת בְּלִי מָ״ה בְּלִי מַהוּת כְּלָל מִשּׁוּם דְּלָאו מִכָּל אִינּוּן מִדּוֹת כְּלָל כו׳ וְהַיְינוּ עַצְמוּת אֵין סוֹף בָּרוּךְ הוּא מַמָּשׁ שֶׁגַּם מַה שֶּׁמְּצַמְצֵם אֶת עַצְמוֹ לִהְיוֹת מָקוֹר לְעֶשֶׂר סְפִירוֹת דַּאֲצִילוּת זֶהוּ רַק הֶאָרָה בְּעָלְמָא הַנִּקְרָא קַו וְחוּט שֶׁנִּמְשָׁךְ מִמַּלְכוּת דְּאֵין סוֹף עַצְמוֹ עַל יְדֵי צִמְצוּם הָרִאשׁוֹן כַּיָּדוּעַ כְּמוֹ מֵאֲצִילוּת לִבְרִיאָה־יְצִירָה־עֲשִׂיָּה מַמָּשׁ כַּנַּ״ל.

וְעַל זֶה אָמַר כִּי עִמְּךָ מְקוֹר כָּל חַיֵּי הָעוֹלָמוֹת דַּאֲצִילוּת־בְּרִיאָה־יְצִירָה־עֲשִׂיָּה כו׳ וְהוּא הַנִּקְרָא סוֹבֵב כָּל עָלְמִין הַכְּלָלִי שֶׁמַּקִּיף לְד׳ עוֹלָמוֹת דַּאֲצִילוּת־בְּרִיאָה־יְצִירָה־עֲשִׂיָּה בְּשָׁוֶה מַמָּשׁ וְזֶהוּ מֶלֶךְ יָחִיד חֵי הָעוֹלָמִים בִּכְלָלוּת הַכֹּל כו׳

When the *tzimtzum* occurred, G-d's Infinite Light was removed and concealed. However, a *reshimah*, an impression of the Light, remained. Subsequently, the *kav*, a thin thread of light, was made to shine through the remaining impression, by way of which the universe was created. This impression is the source of the creation of *keilim* (vessels). Although the *kav* is the aspect of "luminary" and "light," while the *reshimah*, which is latent, is merely the idea of "letters" or "vessels," nevertheless, it is a *reshimah* of the "General Light" which illuminated everywhere before the initial *tzimtzum*, and is not just the contracted light of the *kav*. (*Or Hatorah*, *Bereishit* vol. 7, p. 2386)

183. *Tzimtzum harishon* in Hebrew. See previous footnote.

184. The process of veiling leading to creation (i.e. *tzimtzum*) *starts* at a level which is far lower than the exalted Essence of the Infinite described here.

185. In the plural, for they are all equal.

to include everything. Or, "Only One, life of the *worlds*, King"[186] and "Your Kingship is the Kingship of *all worlds*"[187] on a higher, more general level, as per what was explained above regarding the two levels of *malchut* of *Atzilut*.[188]

YET HIGHER...

Yet higher than this is the level beyond even the general surrounding radiance which subsumes the four worlds of *Aztilut*, *Beriah*, *Yetzirah* and *Asiyah*, at the point of the very Essence and Being of the Divine. (This is called *Supernal Purity*[189] of the Heavens beyond the Heavens.[190] And the main self-surrender in the word *One* is to this very Essence and Being of the Divine, as it says "to You, G-d, I lift my soul"[191]—literally to *You*.)[192]

---

186. Liturgy, *Baruch She-amar*, Morning Service.

187. Psalms 145:13—another verse of *Ashrei*, explained in chapter 4.

188. Here the author has given a second interpretation of the passages from the prayers, showing that they simultaneously concern a far more transcendent level of the Divine: the very Essence, beyond everything, and thus far beyond the interaction between *memale kol almin* and *sovev kol almin* hitherto described. Hence the term *Only One, life of the worlds*: One (Single), which contains, or surrounds all levels of the worlds (plural). The author now

אוֹ יָחִיד חֵי הָעוֹלָמִים מֶלֶךְ וְכֵן מַלְכוּתְךָ מַלְכוּת כָּל עוֹלָמִים בִּכְלָלוּת עַל דֶּרֶךְ הַנַּ"ל בְּב' מַדְרֵיגוֹת בְּמַלְכוּת דַּאֲצִילוּת כו' וְדַי לַמֵּבִין.

וּלְמַעְלָה גַּם מִזֶּה הוּא לְמַעְלָה גַּם מִהְיוֹת בִּבְחִינַת מַקִּיף וְסוֹבֵב כְּלָלִי לַאֲצִילוּת־בְּרִיאָה־יְצִירָה־עֲשִׂיָּה כו' רַק כְּמוֹ שֶׁהוּא בְּמַהוּתוֹ וְעַצְמוּתוֹ מַמָּשׁ (שֶׁנִּקְרָא טְהִירוּ עִלָּאָה שְׁמֵי הַשָּׁמַיִם כו' וְעִיקַּר מְסִירַת נֶפֶשׁ בְּאֶחָד הַיְינוּ לְמַהוּתוֹ וְעַצְמוּתוֹ מַמָּשׁ דַּוְקָא כְּמוֹ שֶׁכָּתוּב אֵלֶיךָ ה' נַפְשִׁי אֶשָּׂא אֵלֶיךָ מַמָּשׁ כַּיָּדוּעַ וְדַי לַמֵּבִין):

proceeds to point out an even higher level of the Infinite Divine.

189. Zohar I:15a. *Tehiru ila'ah* in Hebrew.

190. See Psalms 148:4, Nehemiah 9:6.

191. Psalms 25:1.

192. To summarize: This chapter discussed three distinct categories, or levels: The first, *memale kol almin* and *sovev kol almin*; the second, the general *sovev kol almin*, that surrounds *kol almin*—(lit.) *all* the worlds equally; the third, the Essence of G-d, named *tehiru ila'ah*.

SUMMARY
OF CHAPTER FIVE

The previous chapter describes the inner transformation of the Animal Soul and its natural passions. The passions are now focused on love of G-d instead of their natural material concerns. This occurs through contemplation on the G-dly radiance that creates all the worlds, which triggers inspiration in one's physical heart to love G-d *with all your heart*—"*with both your inclinations*." This *hitbonenut* is within one's reach since it deals with empirical matters. It can actually transform one's heated heart to purity by an inspiration from on High—similar to the radiance of *malchut* on the celestial worlds and angels.

This parallels the burning wick, which is swiftly consumed, yet during its short-lived existence incinerates all alien desires. (*Malchut* too, when it descends into the worlds, and is termed *dark radiance*, abnegates the self to the Divine *Ayin*—including the seventy heavenly princes.) This is achieved even though it is by way of revelation from on High. The verse says of the wicked, *the lamp of the wicked sputters*—it does not grasp the wick [even with a revelation from on High]; but regarding *tzaddikim*, *the light of the righteous rejoices*. (A body in which the radiance of the soul does not shine should be "beaten"—this beating may include troubles regarding children, health or livelihood—and inspires one to an enthusiastic love and fear of G-d. Hence *sputter* vs. *the light*—the *three totally impure kelipot* vs. *kelipat nogah*, a mixture of good and evil.)

But *the illuminating radiance*—the higher form of contemplation, is in *Havaya*. This is in the ten *sefirot* of *Atzilut*, which are united with the Essence—beyond the stage in which *malchut* is a source for *By'a*, transcending even the ray that becomes the source for the ten *sefirot* of *Atzilut*, about which it is stated *You are One but not in the numerical sense*—*tehiru ila'ah*, Heaven beyond the Heavens.

So just as oil reveals the two colors in the flame [bearing in mind the twofold benefit], likewise the spiritual oil—the two kinds of *hitbonenut*—reveals the two levels of Divine service of the soul: 1) *yichuda tata'ah*—transforming the negative enthusiasm to a G-dly one ["going against one's nature"]; 2) *yichuda ila'ah*—uniting with one's source that transcends all of Creation, ultimately G-d's Essence ["a pure radiance"].

INTRODUCTION TO CHAPTER SIX

Through the intense contemplation on the highest levels, as described in chapter 5, one achieves the illumination of the "bright flame" of one's inner spiritual lamp. However, how is it possible to reach such heights through contemplation? Surely thought cannot grasp the Essence of the Divine?

The answer R. DovBer gives is that through the actual performance of *mitzvot*, one in fact *does* connect with the Essence, because the Divine Essence is the source of the *mitzvot*, and it is the Divine Essence that commands us to obey them. Since, in the words of *Sefer Yetzirah*, "the beginning is lodged in the end," only through the Commandments (the "end") is the Essence (the "beginning") revealed.

This leads to the explanation of the fifth aspect of the physical lamp: the vessel of the lamp which holds everything else. This corresponds to the *mitzvot* in general, while the oil expresses the *action* of the *mitzvot* (the selflessness which enables one to carry them out).

6.
REACHING THE ESSENCE

Through intense contemplation concerning the second level of general *sovev* ***kol almin***, which is to surrender one's soul to the pure divine Oneness, one elicits an exalted illumination from the level of *sovev kol almin*, which is [expressed by] *Havaya*. This illumination is the supernal radiance of the "light sown for *tzaddik elyon*,"[193] the bright flame upon the soul of the individual, including that of the smallest soul-spark of Israel. This is the literal meaning of the verse "You are my lamp, O G-d," addressing the Tetragrammaton, and similar verses—"You, *Havaya*, will illuminate my lamp," "When [G-d] shines His light upon my head"[194]—which all refer to this supernal radiance, the actual Name *Havaya* of *Atzilut*.

The Divine illumination shines from that level on each and every person in response to his self-surrender to the pure Divine Oneness, which results from this specific contemplation on *yichuda ila'ah* when reciting the first line of the Shema.

This is called "the light that illuminates," which is actual G-dliness. The words, "and you shall love the L-rd your G-d with all your soul," refer to this level, similar to the verse, "to love the L-rd your G-d… for He is your life,"[195] for this is the source of the life of the radiance of the essence of[196] the soul of all that lives.

HOW IS SUCH CONTEMPLATION POSSIBLE?

However, how is a person able to put his mind and heart into contemplating this general level of *sovev kol almin* which is the Essence of *Ein Sof*, since this is far beyond even the source of the life of the worlds? For "You are exalted beyond all exalted beings…hidden beyond all hidden things…thought does not grasp You at all"[197] (even the Primordial thought of *Adam Kadmon*[198]).

---

193. See chapter 2 above, footnote 28.

194. Job 29:3.

195. Deuteronomy 30:20.

196. Lit., "from where is hewn."

197. *Tikkunei Zohar*, Introduction, 17a.

198. Even the Primordial thought of *Adam*

(ו)

וְהִנֵּה עַל יְדֵי הַעֲמָקַת הַמּוֹחַ וְהַלֵּב הֵיטֵב בְּהִתְבּוֹנְנוּת זֹאת הַשְּׁנִיָּה דִּבְחִינַת סוֹבֵב כָּל עָלְמִין בִּכְלָלוּת וְהוּא לִמְסוֹר נַפְשׁוֹ בְּאַחְדוּת פְּשׁוּטָה מַמָּשׁ כַּנַּ"ל אָז עַל יְדֵי זֶה וַדַּאי יוּמְשַׁךְ מִבְּחִינַת סוֹבֵב כָּל עָלְמִין שֶׁהוּא שֵׁם הוי"ה בִּכְלָל בְּחִינַת אוֹר הָעֶלְיוֹן דִּבְחִינַת אוֹר הַזָּרוּעַ לְצַדִּיק עֶלְיוֹן שֶׁנִּקְרָא נְהוֹרָא חִיוְּורָא עַל נִשְׁמַת הָאָדָם גַּם בְּנִיצוֹץ קָטָן שֶׁבְּיִשְׂרָאֵל וְהוּא מַה שֶּׁכָּתוּב כִּי אַתָּה נֵרִי הוי"ה מַמָּשׁ וְכֵן כִּי אַתָּה תָּאִיר נֵרִי וּכְמוֹ שֶׁכָּתוּב בְּהִלּוֹ נֵרוֹ עֲלֵי רֹאשִׁי דְּקָאֵי הַכֹּל עַל בְּחִינַת אוֹר הָעֶלְיוֹן הַזֶּה שֶׁהוּא בִּבְחִינַת שֵׁם הוי"ה דַּאֲצִילוּת מַמָּשׁ.

שֶׁמִּשָּׁם יָאִיר אוֹר הָאֱלֹקִי עַל כָּל אֶחָד וְאֶחָד בִּמְסִירַת נֶפֶשׁ שֶׁלּוֹ בְּאַחְדוּת פְּשׁוּטָה עַל יְדֵי הִתְבּוֹנְנוּת הַזֹּאת דַּוְקָא בְּיִחוּדָא עִלָּאָה דִּשְׁמַע יִשְׂרָאֵל כו'.

וְהוּא הַנִּקְרָא אוֹר הַמֵּאִיר שֶׁהוּא בְּחִינַת אֱלֹקוּת מַמָּשׁ וְעַל זֶה אָמַר וְאָהַבְתָּ אֵת הוי"ה אֱלֹקֶיךָ בְּכָל נַפְשְׁךָ מַמָּשׁ כו' וּכְמוֹ לְאַהֲבָה אֶת הוי"ה אֱלֹקֶיךָ כִּי הוּא חַיֶּיךָ מַמָּשׁ לְפִי שֶׁמִּשָּׁם מְקוֹר מַחְצַב כָּל חַיֵּי אוֹר הָעַצְמוּת דְּנִשְׁמַת כָּל חַי כו'.

אַךְ אֵיךְ יוּכַל אָדָם לְהַעֲמִיק דַּעְתּוֹ וְלִבּוֹ בְּהִתְבּוֹנְנוּת דְּסוֹבֵב כָּל עָלְמִין הַכְּלָלִי שֶׁהוּא עַצְמוּת אֵין סוֹף בָּרוּךְ הוּא מַמָּשׁ מֵאַחַר שֶׁהוּא לְמַעְלָה מַעְלָה גַּם מִמְּקוֹר כָּל חַיֵּי הָעוֹלָמוֹת כַּנַּ"ל וַהֲרֵי אוֹמֵר דְּאַנְתְּ עִילָּאָה עַל כָּל עִילָּאִין וּסְתִימָא דְּכָל סְתִימִין דְּלֵית מַחֲשָׁבָה תְּפִיסָא בָךְ כְּלָל (אֲפִילוּ מַחֲשָׁבָה הַקְּדוּמָה דְּא"ק [אָדָם קַדְמוֹן] כו').

Kadmon does not grasp the Divine Essence at all.

ADAM KADMON (A"K): Prior to creation, there was only the infinite revelation of G-d that filled all existence—called the *Or Ein Sof.* Within this infinite revelation, limited beings could not possibly exist. Accordingly, there was a progressive lessening and constricting of the *Or Ein Sof,* making room for limited existence.

This progressive constriction, called *tzimt-*

[To explain:] It is known that while in thought and understanding one cannot at all grasp the very essence of the Divine, through one's pure and essential will, one *can* grasp and cleave to and be absorbed in [the Essence], as the verse states, "to cleave to Him."[199] Hence the phrase "[you should love G-d] with all your soul," and other verses, like "my soul longs"[200] and "to You, O G-d, I lift my soul."[201]

PRACTICAL MITZVOT

There is another way that each person can cleave to the essence of the divine, after the intensity of self-surrender with the innermost point of pure will. This is, as it is written [in the Shema], "and these words which I command you today." The term "I" implies "that who I am," referring to the aforementioned general *sovev kol almin*, and also the very Essence, beyond.[202] This is Who "commands you today."

To explain: the very Essence of *Ein Sof* cannot really be revealed below except through practical *mitzvot* in this world, which is at the lowest of all the spiritual levels. This is because "their beginning is lodged in their end"[203]: The beginning of all beginnings is joined to the end of everything—actually performing the *mitzvah*.

---

zum, brought about various planes of reality—referred to as the five worlds. Each "world" is a certain level of concealment of G-dliness, of the *Or Ein Sof*. The highest world (i.e., the one in which there is the least concealment of G-dliness) is called *Adam Kadmon*. It is the primordial world, or the first level of revelation after the *tzimtzum*.

"*Adam*" suggests "in the likeness of," or "in the image of," from the word דומה (*domeh*) in Hebrew); and "*Kadmon*" meaning primordial, or primary. So, *Adam Kadmon* is the primordial world which is "in the likeness of" the infinite light which preceded it and which was concealed in the process of creation. This means that even though *Adam Kadmon* is a world, that is to say it comes into being through the concealment of the Infinite Light (*tzimtzum*), nevertheless, it is such an elevated plane of reality that it is "in the likeness of" the Infinite Light, the *Or Ein Sof*, which precedes (*kadam*) the world of *Adam Kadmon*. Accordingly, *Adam Kadmon* is a level so sublime, pure, and transcendent that it is almost imperceptible.

In Chasidic thought the world of *Adam Kadmon* represents the transcendent will of G-d. The desire that G-d has had that there should be a creation, and what kind of creation it will be, is planned out in one broad, all-encompassing overview, without separation into specific details. This is called the *machshavah hakedumah*, or "primordial thought," of *Adam Kadmon*. The primordial thought functions as the blueprint for all of creation.

All the details of creation, from the beginning of space to the end of space, and the entire six thousand years of creation—are all superimposed in this one thought, for in

הָעִנְיָן יָדוּעַ דִּבְמַחֲשָׁבָה וְהַשָּׂגָה אֵין תְּפִיסָה וְהַשָּׂגָה כְּלָל וּכְלָל בְּמַהוּתוֹ וְעַצְמוּתוֹ יִתְבָּרֵךְ מַמָּשׁ אֲבָל בְּרָצוֹן הַפָּשׁוּט וְעַצְמִי הוּא שֶׁנִּתְפָּס לִהְיוֹת בּוֹ דְּבֵיקוּת וְהִתְכַּלְלוּת מַמָּשׁ כְּמוֹ שֶׁכָּתוּב לְדָבְקָה בוֹ בּוֹ מַמָּשׁ וְהוּא מַה שֶּׁכָּתוּב בְּכָל נַפְשְׁךָ וּכְמוֹ כָּלְתָה נַפְשִׁי כו׳ אֵלֶיךָ ה׳ נַפְשִׁי אֶשָּׂא מַמָּשׁ וְדַי לַמֵּבִין.

וְעוֹד יֵשׁ דָּבָר שֶׁעַל יָדוֹ יִהְיֶה כָּל אֶחָד וְאֶחָד דָּבוּק בְּמַהוּתוֹ וְעַצְמוּתוֹ יִתְבָּרֵךְ אַחַר שֶׁיִּתְפָּעֵל בִּמְסִירַת נֶפֶשׁ בִּנְקוּדַּת הָרָצוֹן הַפָּשׁוּט כַּנַּ״ל וְהוּא בְּמַה שֶּׁכָּתוּב וְהָיוּ הַדְּבָרִים הָאֵלֶּה אֲשֶׁר אָנֹכִי מְצַוְּךָ הַיּוֹם פֵּירוּשׁ אָנֹכִי הוּא מִי שֶׁאָנֹכִי דְּהַיְינוּ בְּחִינַת סוֹבֵב כָּל עָלְמִין הַכְּלָלִי הַנַּ״ל וּלְמַעְלָה מִזֶּה שֶׁהוּא מַהוּתוֹ וְעַצְמוּתוֹ יִתְבָּרֵךְ מַמָּשׁ הוּא אֲשֶׁר אָנֹכִי מְצַוְּךָ הַיּוֹם דַּוְקָא.

וְהָעִנְיָן הוּא לְפִי שֶׁאֵין בְּחִינַת עַצְמוּת אֵין סוֹף בָּרוּךְ הוּא מַמָּשׁ בָּא לִידֵי גִילּוּי לְמַטָּה מַמָּשׁ כִּי אִם עַל יְדֵי מִצְוֹת מַעֲשִׂיּוֹת בָּעוֹלָם הַזֶּה דַּוְקָא שֶׁהוּא סוֹף כָּל הַמַּדְרֵגוֹת הָעֶלְיוֹנוֹת לְפִי שֶׁנָּעוּץ תְּחִלָּתָן בְּסוֹפָן דַּוְקָא דְּהַיְינוּ תְּחִלַּת כָּל הַתְּחִלּוֹת בְּסוֹף הַכֹּל שֶׁהוּא הַמַּעֲשֶׂה דְמִצְוָה בְּפוֹעַל מַמָּשׁ.

Adam Kadmon there is no concept of space and time whatsoever. There is as yet no inside and no outside, no up and no down, no before and no after. There is only a potential for these limitations. Everything is undefined, unified, and simultaneous.

Adam Kadmon is also called the *keter* of all of *seder hishtalshelut* (the chain of being from the very highest world to the very lowest). Just as each individual world begins from *keter*, so too in a general sense—the entire *seder hishtalshelut* begins from the universal *keter*, *Adam Kadmon*.

199. Deuteronomy 11:22.

200. Psalms 84:3.

201. Thus, through intense self-surrender, will-power and longing one *can* connect with the Divine Essence.

202. I.e., the third level, mentioned at the close of chapter 5.

203. See *Sefer Yetzirah* 1:7. The connection between the beginning and the end (or highest and lowest) is not by way of gradual progression; the first cause and final product are not merely the two extremes of the same process. Rather, there is an integral connection between the beginning and end, highest and lowest, such that when the beginning is lodged in the end (and only when it is lodged in the end) it gains the positive qualities of the lowest level in addition to its own. Furthermore, it is only when the final outcome has been accomplished that the original intention inherent within the first cause is realized.

This is called the actual "pathways of G-d,"[204] as the verse, "the end of the matter is... keep G-d's *mitzvot*, for this is all that man is"[205]—the supernal "Man."[206]

(As is known regarding "let not the wise person be praised [on account of his own wisdom] but in this let him be praised: by knowing Me"—literally—"and by doing kindness and justice and charity in the land,"[207] particularly, "for this is what I desire"[208]—with G-d's ultimate desire and will.)

Hence [the verse in the Shema]: "which I"—literally, G-d's very Essence—"command you today." Through actually performing *mitzvot*, He is revealed; and this takes place "today," in this world, as the Sages said: "today [is the time] to do them."[209]

It is not enough to observe the *mitzvot* just in a spiritual form, by [merely contemplating the] *yichuda ila'ah* in supernal worlds. They must actually be physically performed.

WHY PRACTICAL MITZVOT?

This is because the celestial worlds come [into being] by way of *seder hishtalshelut*[210] of *ilah* and *alul*,[211] from the radiance of *Ein Sof* through a process of multiple veiling, as is known. On account of

---

204. Psalms 25:10.

205. Ecclesiastes 12:13.

206. Through the practical *mitzvot* one connects with the essence of G-d.

207. I.e., the observance of the *mitzvot*.

208. Jeremiah 9:22-23.

209. I.e., one must perform the *mitzvot* today, in this world, and tomorrow, in the World to Come, one is to receive the reward for them. See Talmud, *Eruvin* 22a, commenting on Deuteronomy 7:11.

210. SEDER HISHTALSHELUT: Lit. "Order of Progression of Worlds," or "Chain of Worlds," meaning the giving of life to the various levels of creation through a process of gradual and ordered descent and downward gradation, by means of numerous contractions of the Divine force.

211. ILAH V'ALUL. The creation of physicality (matter) as *something from nothing* could therefore never have come about by way of *ilah* and *alul*, no matter how many steps separate the final product from the initial cause. This is because the final *alul* is inevitably affected by the original *ilah*. If the *ilah* is some spiritual level, the final product can be nothing more than a less refined form of spirituality. Moreover, the final *alul* is initially contained within the first *ilah*, if only in an extremely indistinct form. Physical matter, by definition, could never have been contained within spirituality. Matter must therefore be created *ex nihilo* by G-d alone. This is referred to as *yesh m'ayin*—being from nothingness.

Ilah and *alul* thus exist within the same realm, even if the mode of existence of the *ilah* is far more refined than that of the *alul*. Mat-

שֶׁזֶּהוּ הַנִּקְרָא אָרְחוֹת הוי״ה מַמָּשׁ כְּמוֹ שֶׁכָּתוּב סוֹף דָּבָר כו׳ וְאֶת מִצְוֹתָיו שְׁמוֹר כִּי זֶה כָּל הָאָדָם דִּלְעֵילָא.

(וְכַיָּדוּעַ בְּעִנְיַן אַל יִתְהַלֵּל חָכָם כו׳ כִּי אִם בְּזֹאת יִתְהַלֵּל הַמִּתְהַלֵּל הַשְׂכֵּל וְיָדוֹעַ אוֹתִי מַמָּשׁ לַעֲשׂוֹת חֶסֶד וּמִשְׁפָּט וּצְדָקָה בָּאָרֶץ דַּוְקָא כִּי בְאֵלֶּה חָפַצְתִּי בְּחֵפֶץ וְרָצוֹן הַקָּדוּם מַמָּשׁ כו׳).

וְזֶהוּ אֲשֶׁר אָנֹכִי מַמָּשׁ בְּחִינַת מַהוּתוֹ וְעַצְמוּתוֹ מְצַוְּךָ הַיּוֹם בְּמִצְוֹת בְּפוֹעַל מַמָּשׁ הוּא מִתְגַּלֶּה דַּוְקָא וְהַיּוֹם בָּעוֹלָם הַזֶּה דַּוְקָא כְּמוֹ שֶׁאָמְרוּ זִכְרוֹנָם לִבְרָכָה הַיּוֹם לַעֲשׂוֹתָם כו׳.

וְלֹא כְּמוֹ שֶׁהֵן בְּרוּחָנִיּוּת בְּיִחוּדָא עִלָּאָה בְּעוֹלָמוֹת עֶלְיוֹנִים אֶלָּא בְּסוֹף מַעֲשֶׂה בְּפוֹעַל מַמָּשׁ בְּגַשְׁמִיּוּת דַּוְקָא.

וְהוּא לְפִי שֶׁעוֹלָמוֹת עֶלְיוֹנִים הֲרֵי הֵן בָּאִים בְּסֵדֶר הַהִשְׁתַּלְשְׁלוּת עִילָּה וְעָלוּל מֵאוֹר אֵין סוֹף בָּרוּךְ הוּא עַל יְדֵי רִיבּוּי צִימְצוּמִים כַּיָּדוּעַ שֶׁמִּפְּנֵי זֶה וַדַּאי אִי אֶפְשָׁר

---

ter, however, does not exist within the realm of the spiritual at all. Its source is therefore called *ayin*—"nothingness"—relative to the mode of being and perception of the *yesh* (the physical being). The coming into existence of the *yesh* is for this reason called *hitchadshut*—originality or innovativeness—since it did not exist at all prior to its creation (*Sefer HaMaamarim 5700*, pp. 121-3).

Although the final *alul* is of the same realm as the original *ilah*, and is therefore similar to it, it is not dependent upon it for its existence. On the contrary, once the *alul* has been produced it continues to exist, even if the *ilah* no longer exists—just as a vessel continues to exist even if its maker has since left. By contrast, the existence of the *yesh* is always dependent upon the *ayin* bringing it into being, since it has no independent existence (*Sefer HaMaamarim 5701*, pp. 8-9). In this sense the *yesh* may be compared to a ray of sunshine that is produced by the sun. If the sun were to suddenly be extinguished, the ray would cease to exist, for it exists only by virtue of the sun's radiant nature (See *Tanya*, *Sha'ar HaYichud v'haEmunah*, ch. 3).

The relationship between *ilah* (cause) and *alul* (effect) is such that the *alul* is contained within the *ilah*—albeit in an undefined state—even before the *alul* emerges into being. The ilah *produces* the *alul*; it does not *create* it. Thus, the *alul's* emergence is not a creation of a new being, since it is merely a *revelation* from within the *ilah* where it was "hidden," i.e., undefined.

For example: When a person ponders some goal, he develops a desire to achieve it. Contemplating the goal is the *ilah*; the resulting desire is the *alul*. Furthermore, as the person acts upon his motivation (so that the motivation becomes the immediate *ilah* and the action the *alul*), the original *ilah* still affects the final *alul*, albeit from a greater "distance." (*Sefer HaLikutim*, *Ilah V'Alul*, p. 221-2, 226).

this it is clearly impossible that anything of the Divine Essence should be revealed in them, for [even human] "thought cannot grasp Him at all," as mentioned above. The only way the Essence *can* be revealed is not through the process of *hishtalshelut* of *ilah* and *alul*, but in a manner of [direct] descent and investment, as in the actual physical performance of the *mitzvot*. Only this can elicit [the Essence] to be manifest in this world.[212]

Because of the great exaltedness of the radiance of *Ein Sof* itself, it cannot flow to the worlds by way of *hishtalshelut* at all, and can only come in a manner of direct investment. There is a general rule that whatever is higher is more able to descend to a lower point, as it says "He rises up... and descends below,"[213] and also, "I am exalted [yet dwell with the crushed"].[214] Similarly, "what is the House [which you can build for Me],"[215] for "the Heavens and the heavens of the heavens cannot hold"[216] Him, and nonetheless He contracted His Divine Presence between the staves of the ark[217] in the physical space of the Temple.[218] Similarly regarding the investment of the very radiance of the *Ein Sof* in the actual performance of every *mitzvah*.

Thus it is written, "which I command you today"—specifically *today* [in this world] and not tomorrow in the World to Come.[219]

THE FIFTH ASPECT OF THE LAMP

(This [concept of the *mitzvot*] is the fifth aspect, in addition to the other four aspects of the lamp: the vessel of the lamp itself, which contains everything. Thus, the verse states, "For a lamp is the *mitzvah*, and the Torah is light."[220] The lamp contains the whole essence

---

212. The action of the *mitzvot* provides a direct channel of expression of the Essence of G-d. This contrasts with the step-by-step process of descent through the spiritual realms, with veiling of the spiritual energy at each stage of the process. The *mitzvot* cause the Essence of G-d to be directly vested within creation, bypassing the step-by-step descent.

PHYSICALITY AS THE VESSEL FOR ESSENCE. In *Samach T'samach 5657*, Rabbi Shalom DovBer offers four examples illustrating the idea that the vessel for the sublime must be material and crude and that it cannot be contained by the spiritual and refined: 1) A truly deep concept can only be conveyed by means of a gross analogy. A moderately deep concept can be conveyed without an analogy. 2) The rays of the sun can only be discerned in the coarse atmosphere of Earth. Beyond Earth, the delicate and refined air makes the sun's rays imperceptible. 3) Sight, which is a loftier sense than hearing, apprehends coarse physicality. Hearing, a lower faculty, apprehends intangible sound. 4) In Ezekiel's vision of the *merkavah*, the supernal "chariot," the face of the lion is to the right while the face of the ox

שֶׁיִּתְגַּלֶּה בָּהֶם מִבְּחִינַת מַהוּתוֹ וְעַצְמוּתוֹ יִתְבָּרֵךְ מַמָּשׁ בְּגִילּוּי דְּלֵית מַחֲשָׁבָה תְּפִיסָא בֵיהּ כְּלָל כַּנַ"ל רַק שֶׁלֹּא בְּדֶרֶךְ הִשְׁתַּלְשְׁלוּת עִילָּה וְעָלוּל אֶלָּא בְּדֶרֶךְ יְרִידָה וְהִתְלַבְּשׁוּת לְבָד כְּמוֹ בְּמַעֲשֵׂה הַמִּצְוֹת בְּפוֹעַל מַמָּשׁ בְּגַשְׁמִיּוּת דַּוְקָא הוּא שֶׁיָּכוֹל לָבֹא לְמַטָּה בְּגִלּוּי.

כִּי לְעוֹצֶם רוֹמְמוּת עֶרֶךְ הָאוֹר דְּאֵין סוֹף עַצְמוֹ לֹא יָבֹא בְּדֶרֶךְ הִשְׁתַּלְשְׁלוּת כְּלָל כִּי אִם בְּדֶרֶךְ הִתְלַבְּשׁוּת לְמַטָּה דַּוְקָא שֶׁלֹּא בְּהַדְרָגָה כְּלָל וְכַיָּדוּעַ הַכְּלָל בְּכָל מָקוֹם שֶׁכֹּל הַגָּבוֹהַּ גָּבוֹהַּ יוֹתֵר יוֹתֵר יוּכַל לָבֹא בִּירִידָה בְּמָקוֹם הַיּוֹתֵר נָמוּךְ דַּוְקָא וּכְמוֹ שֶׁכָּתוּב הַמַּגְבִּיהִי לָשָׁבֶת הַמַּשְׁפִּילִי כו' וּכְתִיב אֲנִי מָרוֹם כו' וְכֵן אוֹמֵר אֵיזֶה בַיִת אֲשֶׁר כו' כִּי הַשָּׁמַיִם וּשְׁמֵי הַשָּׁמַיִם לֹא יְכַלְכְּלוּהוּ וְעִם כָּל זֶה צִמְצֵם שְׁכִינָתוֹ בֵּין בַּדֵּי הָאָרוֹן בְּהֵיכָל וּמָקוֹם גַּשְׁמִי וְכַךְ הוּא בְּעִנְיַן הִתְלַבְּשׁוּת אוֹר אֵין סוֹף מַמָּשׁ בְּכָל מִצְוָה בְּפוֹעַל מַמָּשׁ.

וְזֶהוּ שֶׁכָּתוּב אֲשֶׁר אָנֹכִי מְצַוְּךָ הַיּוֹם דַּוְקָא וְלֹא לְמָחָר בָּעוֹלָם הַבָּא כו'.

(וְזֶהוּ עִנְיַן דָּבָר הַחֲמִישִׁי הַנּוֹסָף עַל ד' דְּבָרִים שֶׁבְּאוֹר הַנֵּר וְהוּא כְּלִי הַנֵּר עַצְמוֹ הַמַּחֲזִיק הַכֹּל וּכְמוֹ שֶׁכָּתוּב כִּי נֵר מִצְוָה וְתוֹרָה אוֹר הֲרֵי הַנֵּר מַחֲזִיק לְכָל עִיקָּר וּמָקוֹר דְּאוֹר

---

is to the left (which is of lesser stature than the right.) Yet in their physical form, the lion is an impure (non-kosher) animal that ravages its prey while the ox is a pure animal that can be brought as a sacrifice before G-d.

213. Psalms 113:5-6. Because "G-d dwells on high," He is able to "look down so low upon heaven and earth."

214. Isaiah 57:15. Here too, because G-d is exalted, He is able to dwell with the crushed.

215. Ibid. 66:1.

216. I Kings 8:27.

217. *Bereishit Rabbah* 84:4.

218. Thus in these descriptions, the greater G-d is, the more He is able to descend below.

219. It is the physical act of a *mitzvah* that elicits G-d's Essence to descend to this world—hence the importance of actually performing the *mitzvot.*

220. Proverbs 6:23.

and source of the radiance of the Torah, and this is *the light that illuminates*—the revelation of *Havaya,* because their beginning [*Havaya*] is lodged in their end, specifically termed the *lamp of the mitzvah.*)

Now the *physical performance* of Torah and *mitzvot,* which have the power to elicit the revelation of the Divine Essence, so that it illuminates with the radiance of *Havaya* itself, as explained above, is the "oil" which is drawn after the wick. On account of the oil[221] there is the revelation of the spiritual radiance of *the Light which illuminates,*[222] the "bright radiance," which depends on the purity of the oil.[223] This is because the oil is drawn after the wick and attracts the light. From the oil comes the manifestation of the two types of radiance, the "bright radiance" and the "dark radiance."

Thus [the Shema] reads: "And these words"—meaning, specifically the words of Torah, "which I command you today"—meaning, that they be physically performed. (As it continues "you shall teach them diligently [to your children]… you shall bind them [as *tefillin*]"—which includes the physical performance of all the *mitzvot,* as is known.)

---

221. I.e., Torah and *mitzvot.*

222. I.e., G-d's Essence.

תּוֹרָה שֶׁזֶּהוּ בְּחִינַת אוֹר הַמֵּאִיר שֶׁהוּא גִלּוּי אוֹר הוי"ה מַמָּשׁ כַּנַּ"ל לְפִי שֶׁנָּעוּץ תְּחִלָּתָן בְּסוֹפָן דַּוְקָא שֶׁהוּא הַכְּלִי שֶׁנִּקְרָא נֵר מִצְוָה דַּוְקָא וְדַי לַמֵּבִין).

וְהִנֵּה בְּחִינַת הַמַּעֲשֶׂה בְּתוֹרָה וּמִצְוֹת שֶׁבְּכֹחָם יֵשׁ לְהַמְשִׁיךְ גִּילּוּי מַהוּתוֹ וְעַצְמוּתוֹ יִתְבָּרֵךְ לְהָאִיר אוֹר דְּשֵׁם הוי"ה מַמָּשׁ כַּנַּ"ל הוּא בְּחִינַת הַשֶּׁמֶן שֶׁנִּמְשָׁךְ אַחַר הַפְּתִילָה שֶׁמֵּחֲמָתוֹ דַּוְקָא יָבֹא גִלּוּי אוֹר הָעֶלְיוֹן דְּאוֹר הַמֵּאִיר שֶׁנִּקְרָא נְהוֹרָא חִוְּורָא שֶׁהוּא לְפִי עֶרֶךְ צְלִילַת הַשֶּׁמֶן כַּנַּ"ל לְפִי שֶׁנִּשְׁאָב בַּפְּתִילָה וּמוֹשֵׁךְ אֶת הָאוֹר כו' וְכַנַּ"ל דְּמִן הַשֶּׁמֶן בָּא לְגִלּוּי ב' גַּוְונֵי אוֹר הַלָּלוּ דִּנְהוֹרָא חִוְּורָא וְנְהוֹרָא אוּכָּמָא כו'.

וְהַיְינוּ מַה שֶּׁכָּתוּב וְהָיוּ הַדְּבָרִים הָאֵלֶּה דַּוְקָא שֶׁהוּא דִּבְרֵי הַתּוֹרָה אֲשֶׁר אָנֹכִי מְצַוְּךָ הַיּוֹם שֶׁיָּבוֹאוּ בְּפוֹעַל מַמָּשׁ כו' (וּכְמוֹ שֶׁכָּתוּב וְשִׁנַּנְתָּם כו' וּקְשַׁרְתָּם כו' שֶׁהוּא כּוֹלֵל כָּל מַעֲשֵׂה הַמִּצְוֹת דַּוְקָא כַּיָּדוּעַ):

223. I.e., dependent on how well one performs Torah and *mitzvot*.

SUMMARY
OF CHAPTER SIX

Through intense contemplation on the highest levels—*yichuda ila'ah*, as described in chapter 5, one draws a Supernal radiance into one's inner spirit, so *You— Havaya* itself—*will be my lamp*. This is the *bright radiance* of *yichuda ila'ah* of Shema Yisrael, to cause *You shall love [G-d]...with all your soul* since it is from there that the entire life of the radiance of the essence of the soul of every living being is hewn. The question is asked, however, since this contemplation deals with matters that transcend soul-life, how is it possible to reach such heights through contemplation?

The answer is that it can be done in a twofold manner: 1) Though one cannot attain this level through contemplation, it can be attained by subduing one's essential will to want to cleave to G-d, for will transcends intellect; 2) through the practical *mitzvot* one in fact *does* connect with the Essence, since the Divine Essence transcends the three parts of intellect [*chochmah*, *binah*, *daat*]. Hence the verse, *And these words which I* ("whoever I am," His Essence) *command you today*, for today, i.e., this terrestrial world, is the arena for the performance of *mitzvot*. Since *Ein Sof* is so infinitely exalted, its revelation cannot be in a manner of *hishtalshelut* of *ilah* and *alul*, but rather only by vesting in Torah and *mitzvot*. For whatever is of a more sublime source, can be manifest in a lower level.

(This explains the vessel of the lamp, which holds the oil and the wick, the source for all the radiance in all its colors. [The vessel corresponds to the *mitzvot* in general, while the oil refers to the *action* of the *mitzvot*—the selflessness that enables one to carry them out.])

So although one attains spiritual oil (*hitbonenut*) with which to produce a well-structured flame, it must rest in a vessel (*mitzvot*) to function as a lamp.

INTRODUCTION TO CHAPTER SEVEN

R. DovBer cites another verse from *Ashrei* (Psalm 145) that helps explain the power of Torah and *mitzvot* in connecting the person to the Divine Essence: "G-d is close to all who call Him, to all who call Him in truth."

"Truth" refers to the Divine Essence, vested in Torah and *mitzvot.* Through Torah and *mitzvot,* G-d is equally near to every Jew. With prayer, however, in which one comes close to G-d, many different levels exist, varying according to the spiritual root of one's soul.

Thus one can understand the verse "Let us make Man in our Form and in our Image." Through Torah the Jew attains the Divine Form, and through *mitzvot,* the Divine Image. This also relates to the theme of a lamp, through the verse "For the *mitzvah* is a lamp and the Torah is light."

7.
TORAH, MITZVOT AND PRAYER

G-D IS CLOSE TO ALL (THROUGH TORAH AND MITZVOT)

Hence [the verse in *Ashrei*], "G-d is close to all who call upon Him, to all who call upon Him in truth." The word "close" means that He is close to all, equally, whether small or great, without any distinction of levels at all. Thus it says "to all who call Him"—whoever they may be, as long as they call upon Him "in truth."

This means calling upon Him as He is in the truth of His Essence, the ultimate *sovev kol almin* described above, which is utterly beyond the realm of *histalshelut ilah* and *alul.* The only way this level of the Essence is expressed is by being vested in Torah and *mitzvot* in the "final realm" of actual performance. This is how He is close to all who call upon Him, meaning to the one who reads[224] the Torah, as the verse [in the Shema], "and these words... shall be [on your heart]... and you shall speak of them."

By studying Torah one calls upon the very Essence of the Divine, which is far beyond the entire *histalshelut* of *Atzilut*, *Beriah*, *Yetzirah* and *Asiyah*. This is calling "in truth": "There is no truth but Torah,"[225] for this refers to the truth of the Divine Essence, before Whom small and great are equal, and Who is close to all without any distinction whatsoever.

DISTINCTIONS IN PRAYER

Quite different is the calling and crying [to G-d] in prayer. Although the verse states, "who is like the L-rd our G-d, in all our calling to Him"[226]—specifically [to His Essence], as in the verse "to You O G-d, I lift my soul," to His very Essence—nonetheless, through this He does not come totally close to everyone equally. Rather, [G-d comes close] to each person according to his measure of preparation in his heart, mind and will, as the verse says "focusing one's heart [on G-d]."[227] And

224. *Koray*, translated as "read" or "study," can also be translated as "call."

225. See Jerusalem Talmud, *Rosh Hashanah* 3:8.

226. Deuteronomy 4:7.

227. Job 34:14. The full verse reads, "Were He to set His heart upon man, He could gather his spirit and his soul unto Himself," i.e.,

(ז)

וְזֶהוּ קָרוֹב ה׳ לְכָל קוֹרְאָיו לְכֹל אֲשֶׁר יִקְרָאוּהוּ בֶאֱמֶת פֵּירוּשׁ קָרוֹב שֶׁהוּא קָרוֹב לַכֹּל בְּשָׁוֶה לַקָּטֹן כַּגָּדוֹל בְּלִי חִילּוּק מַדְרֵגוֹת כְּלָל וְזֶהוּ לְכָל קוֹרְאָיו יִהְיֶה מִי שֶׁיִּהְיֶה וְהַיְינוּ לְכֹל אֲשֶׁר יִקְרָאוּהוּ בֶאֱמֶת דַּוְקָא.

שֶׁזֶּהוּ כְּמוֹ שֶׁהוּא בַּאֲמִתַּת עַצְמוּתוֹ שֶׁהוּא בְּחִינַת סוֹבֵב כָּל עָלְמִין הַנַּ״ל שֶׁאֵינוֹ בָּא בְּדֶרֶךְ הִשְׁתַּלְשְׁלוּת עִלָּה וְעָלוּל כְּלָל רַק בָּא בְּדֶרֶךְ בְּחִינַת הִתְלַבְּשׁוּת בְּתוֹרָה וּמִצְוֹת בְּסוֹף מַעֲשֶׂה דַּוְקָא כַּנַּ״ל בָּזֶה הֲרֵי הוּא קָרוֹב לְכָל קוֹרְאָיו וְהוּא הַקּוֹרֵא בַּתּוֹרָה כְּמוֹ שֶׁכָּתוּב וְהָיוּ הַדְּבָרִים הָאֵלֶּה כו׳ וְדִבַּרְתָּ בָּם כו׳.

שֶׁקּוֹרֵא לִבְחִינַת מַהוּתוֹ וְעַצְמוּתוֹ יִתְבָּרֵךְ מַמָּשׁ שֶׁלְּמַעְלָה מֵעְלָה מִכָּל הַהִשְׁתַּלְשְׁלוּת דַּאֲצִילוּת־בְּרִיאָה־יְצִירָה־עֲשִׂיָּה כַּנַּ״ל וְזֶהוּ בֶּאֱמֶת אֵין אֱמֶת אֶלָּא תוֹרָה שֶׁהוּא אֲמִתַּת עַצְמוּתוֹ יִתְבָּרֵךְ שֶׁשָּׁוֶה לְפָנָיו קָטֹן וְגָדוֹל וְקָרוֹב הוּא לְכוּלָּם בְּשָׁוֶה מַמָּשׁ.

מַה שֶּׁאֵין כֵּן הַקְּרִיאָה וְהַצְּעָקָה בִּתְפִלָּה שֶׁאַף עַל פִּי שֶׁנֶּאֱמַר מִי כַּה׳ אֱלֹקֵינוּ בְּכָל קָרְאֵינוּ אֵלָיו דַּוְקָא כְּמוֹ אֵלֶיךָ ה׳ נַפְשִׁי אֶשָּׂא כו׳ לִבְחִינַת מַהוּתוֹ וְעַצְמוּתוֹ מַמָּשׁ כַּנַּ״ל אֲבָל אֵינוֹ בָּא לִכְלַל קֵירוּב גָּמוּר לַכֹּל בְּשָׁוֶה אֶלָּא לְכָל אֶחָד כְּפוּם שִׁיעוּרָא דִּילֵיהּ בַּהֲכָנַת לִבּוֹ וְדַעְתּוֹ וּרְצוֹנוֹ כו׳ כְּמוֹ

"If G-d were to focus upon man's actions, he would not survive G-d's examination of him." Kabbalah translates the verse to connote man's motivation towards G-d: "If man set his heart unto G-d," i.e., if *man* physically sets his heart to (love and fear) *G-d*—"he will gather *G-d's* spirit and *G-d's* soul unto himself," i.e., he arouses G-d's benevolence towards him. See *Zohar* II:162b; III: 177a; *Torah Or*, 1a ff.; 121d, for an elaboration on this meaning.

even then, "from a distance G-d appears to me,"[228] and not truly close.

All this is because even the Supernal Radiance of *sovev kol almin*, which is elicited through the contemplation of *Shema Yisrael* and the ecstasy of the words "and you should love [G-d]... with all your heart and with all your soul," has to come by way of an influence from above to below. It comes in a way of *hishtalshelut*, reaching each person according to his root in the ten *sefirot* of *By'a*, according to the different levels of his *nefesh, ruach* or *neshamah*,[229] which are rooted in the externality of the vessels of *Atzilut* as is known.[230] This flow dwells on each person, encompassing him from a distance; hence the verse, "from a distance G-d appears to me."

This applies to every [level of] radiance, even the highest, when it descends step-by-step through stages—named *histalshelut*. However, when the very same level of supernal radiance is expressed through being vested in Torah and *mitzvot*, then it is truly "close" to all, small as well as great equally, as the verse, "call upon Him when He is close"[231]—by means of Torah and *mitzvot*. ["Close" is related to Torah and *mitzvot*] as it is written "for the thing is very near to you, in your mouth and in your heart to perform it"[232]—specifically, and it is not in Heaven.[233] And this [observance of Torah and *mitzvot*] is "what I command you," as was explained above.[234]

"FORM" AND "IMAGE"

This explains the verse, "let us make man in our form and our image"[235]—referring specifically to Torah and *mitzvot*: As is known, the

---

228. Jeremiah 31:2.

229. NEFESH, RUACH, NESHAMAH (CHAYA, YECHIDA): See *Bereishit Rabbah* 14:9; *Devarim Rabbah* 2:37: Five names are given to the soul—*Nefesh*, *Ruach*, *Neshama*, *Chaya*, *Yechida*. In some editions of the Midrash and liturgical hymns, there are changes in this order. But in the writings of the Arizal and in Chasidic literature this order specifically is stated. See *Zohar* I:81a; 206a.

These five names are the five levels of the soul. In rough translation: *Nefesh* ("Vitality") is the lowest grade and life-force of the body, the natural soul and simple life of man. *Ruach* ("Spirit"), the next grade, is the spiritual faculty vivifying man's emotional attributes. *Neshama* ("Soul") is the Divine Force vivifying the intellect. *Chaya* ("Living") is an even more refined G-dly level. *Yechida* is the Divine spark itself clothed in the most refined spark of the soul. *Yechida* is the innermost point of the soul, "united" and one with G-d. It represents total *bittul*, self-nullification, nothingness. Since every one of Israel possesses each of the five, four obscure and one pre-

שֶׁכָּתוּב אִם יָשִׂים אֵלָיו לִבּוֹ כו׳ וְגַם זֶה מֵרָחוֹק ה׳ נִרְאָה לִי וְלֹא בְּקֵירוּב גָּמוּר.

וְכָל זֶה מִפְּנֵי שֶׁגַּם זֶה הָאוֹר הָעֶלְיוֹן דִּבְחִינַת סוֹבֵב כָּל עָלְמִין הַבָּא עַל יְדֵי הִתְבּוֹנְנוּת דִּשְׁמַע יִשְׂרָאֵל כו׳ וְהִתְפַּעֲלוּת דִּוְאָהַבְתָּ בְּכָל לְבָבְךָ וְנַפְשְׁךָ כו׳ צָרִיךְ לָבֹא בְּדֶרֶךְ הַשְׁפָּעָה מִלְמַעְלָה לְמַטָּה שֶׁהוּא בָּא בְּדֶרֶךְ הַהִשְׁתַּלְשְׁלוּת עַד כָּל אֶחָד בְּשָׁרְשׁוֹ בְּעֶשֶׂר סְפִירוֹת דִּבְרִיאָה־יְצִירָה־עֲשִׂיָּה בְּחִילּוּק הַמַּדְרֵיגוֹת דְּנֶפֶשׁ־רוּחַ־נְשָׁמָה שֶׁשָּׁרְשָׁם בְּחִיצוֹנִיּוּת הַכֵּלִים דַּאֲצִילוּת כַּיָּדוּעַ וְשׁוֹרֶה עַל כָּל אֶחָד וְאֶחָד בִּבְחִינַת מַקִּיף מֵרָחוֹק וְזֶהוּ שֶׁנֶּאֱמַר מֵרָחוֹק ה׳ נִרְאָה לִי כו׳.

שֶׁזֶּהוּ בְּכָל אוֹר גַּם הַיּוֹתֵר עֶלְיוֹן כַּאֲשֶׁר בָּא בִּירִידוֹת הַמַּדְרֵיגוֹת עַל כָּל פָּנִים כו׳ שֶׁנִּקְרָא הִשְׁתַּלְשְׁלוּת מַה שֶּׁאֵין כֵּן הָאוֹר הָעֶלְיוֹן זֶה עַצְמוֹ כְּשֶׁבָּא בִּבְחִינַת הִתְלַבְּשׁוּת בְּתוֹרָה וּמִצְוֹת קָרוֹב הוּא מַמָּשׁ לַכֹּל כַּקָּטֹן כַּגָּדוֹל מַמָּשׁ בְּשָׁוֶה וּכְמוֹ שֶׁנֶּאֱמַר קְרָאוּהוּ בִּהְיוֹתוֹ קָרוֹב עַל יְדֵי תוֹרָה וּמִצְוֹת וּכְמוֹ שֶׁכָּתוּב כִּי קָרוֹב אֵלֶיךָ הַדָּבָר מְאֹד בְּפִיךָ וּבִלְבָבְךָ לַעֲשׂוֹתוֹ דַּוְקָא וְלֹא בַשָּׁמַיִם הִיא כו׳ וְהוּא הַדָּבָר אֲשֶׁר אָנֹכִי מְצַוְּךָ כו׳ מִטַּעַם הַנַּ״ל בְּפֵירוּשׁ אָנֹכִי מְצַוְּךָ כַּנַּ״ל.

וְזֶהוּ עִנְיַן נַעֲשֶׂה אָדָם בְּצַלְמֵנוּ כִּדְמוּתֵינוּ כו׳ וְקָאֵי הַכֹּל

---

dominant, *Yechida* in this sense is expressed in *mesirat nefesh*—literal self-sacrifice, martyrdom if need be.

David, Elijah, Moses, Adam, and Moshiach, each possess the general level of each of these five categories. Moshiach possesses the general *Yechida* of all souls.

230. The ultimate source of the G-dly soul is very exalted. However, it manifests itself in the person in a more limited way, relating to levels within the three worlds of *By'a* which themselves relate back to the vessels of the *sefirot* of *Atzilut*. See *Likkutei Torah, Shir HaShirim* 19c; *Derushim L'Yom HaKippurim* 70c.

231. Isaiah 55:6.

232. Deuteronomy 30:14. This verse refers to observance of Torah and *mitzvot*, and calls them "close."

233. Ibid. 30:12. I.e., beyond reach, see Talmud, *Bava Metzia* 59b.

234. Chapter 6 (*PRACTICAL MITZVOT*).

235. Genesis 1:26.

explanation of the verse "a lamp is the *mitzvah*, and the Torah is light"[236] is, that the root of Torah is the radiance [of the *sefirot*] and that of the *mitzvah* is the vessel,[237] and in several places the verse states, "the Torah and the *mitzvah*"[238]—meaning the "form" and "image." "Form" signifies the male, and "image" signifies the female. These two levels correspond to *sovev kol almin* and *memale kol almin*, respectively, in the [general kabbalistic depiction] of *hishtalshelut*.

And just as the "form" is the essential shape [of all existence], all the ten *sefirot* of *Atzilut* consist of *ohr* and *keli* [i.e. form and image], like "*chesed*, the right arm,[239] and *chochmah*...the *brain*."[240]

This [pattern of the *sefirot*] is actually "in Our [i.e. in G-d's] form"—*Havaya* of *Atzilut*,[241] and emerges through the light of Torah, as the verses, "these words [which I command you],"[242] and, "This is the Torah of Man,"[243] implying the inwardness of the *orot* and *keilim* of the Supernal Man [—the *sefirot*]. Hence the Torah is termed "the Torah of *Havaya*," literally.[244]

The term "in our image" expresses the feminine.[245] This is the aspect of *malchut*, which is called "the *appearance* of the image of the Glory of G-d"[246] of *Ein Sof*, as in the verse "I [G-d] shall make myself known to him in a *vision*"[247]; and as in "the prophets will conceive *images* for Me."[248] This is like an image which bears the impression of the essential form, the *tzelem*. The image constitutes the practical *mitzvot* which descend to this world, and are called *mitzvot of the king*, and they receive [the imprint of the *form*].

This "image" is termed the *lamp of the mitzvah*—and although it is also called *the mitzvah of Havaya*[249]—yet, [the "image"] is man-

---

236. Discussed in the previous chapter.

237. The *sefirot* are described as spiritual radiance within vessels. See footnote 279.

238. E.g., Exodus 24:12.

239. In *Patach Eliyahu* (*Tikkunei Zohar, Introduction II*) the *sefirot* are depicted as corresponding to various limbs of the human body: *chesed* to the right hand, *gevurah* to the left hand, etc.

240. The spiritual attribute—"form"— e.g, *chesed*, is expressed through an "image," the right arm. Likewise, the "form" of *chochmah* is expressed through the "image" of the brain.

241. The *yud* is *chochmah*, the *hey* is *binah*, the *vav* signifies the six *sefirot* from *chesed* to *yesod* and the second *hey* is *malchut*.

242. This phrase from the Shema signifies the Torah.

בְּתוֹרָה וּמִצְוֹת דַּוְקָא כַּיָּדוּעַ בְּעִנְיַן נֵר מִצְוָה וְתוֹרָה אוֹר שֶׁשֹּׁרֶשׁ הַתּוֹרָה הוּא בְּאוֹר וְהַמִּצְוָה בִּכְלִי וּכְמוֹ שֶׁכָּתוּב בְּכַמָּה מְקוֹמוֹת הַתּוֹרָה וְהַמִּצְוָה כו׳ שֶׁזֶּהוּ עִנְיַן צֶלֶם וּדְמוּת וְכַיָּדוּעַ שֶׁצֶּלֶם בִּדְכוּרָא וּדְמוּת בְּנוּקְבָא שֶׁהוּא בְּחִינַת סוֹבֵב וּמְמַלֵּא בְּעִנְיַן הַהִשְׁתַּלְשְׁלוּת כַּנַּ״ל.

כְּמוֹ שֶׁהַצֶּלֶם הוּא בְּחִינַת צוּרָה הָעַצְמִית כָּךְ כָּל עֶשֶׂר סְפִירוֹת דַּאֲצִילוּת בְּאוֹרוֹת וְכֵלִים כְּמוֹ חֶסֶד דְּרוֹעָא כו׳ חָכְמָה מוֹחָא כו׳.

זֶהוּ בְּצַלְמֵנוּ מַמָּשׁ דְּהַיְינוּ בְּשֵׁם הוי״ה דַּאֲצִילוּת וְהוּא עַל יְדֵי בְּחִינַת אוֹר דְּתוֹרָה כְּמוֹ שֶׁכָּתוּב וְהָיוּ הַדְּבָרִים הָאֵלֶּה כו׳ שֶׁנֶּאֱמַר וְזֹאת תּוֹרַת הָאָדָם מַמָּשׁ בִּבְחִינָה פְּנִימִית דְּאוֹרוֹת וְכֵלִים דְּאָדָם הָעֶלְיוֹן וְעַל כֵּן נִקְרָא תּוֹרַת הוי״ה מַמָּשׁ.

וּדְמוּתֵינוּ בְּנוּקְבָא הוּא בִּבְחִינַת מַלְכוּת שֶׁנִּקְרָא מַרְאֵה דְּמוּת כְּבוֹד הוי״ה דְּאֵין סוֹף כְּמוֹ ה׳ בַּמַּרְאָה אֵלָיו אֶתְוַדָּע וְכֵן בְּיַד הַנְּבִיאִים אֲדַמֶּה כו׳ וְהוּא כְּמוֹ הַדְּמוּת שֶׁנֶּחְקַק בּוֹ צוּרָה הָעַצְמִית הַנִּקְרָא צֶלֶם וְהֵן הֵנָּה הַמִּצְוֹת מַעֲשִׂיּוֹת שֶׁבָּאִים לְמַטָּה שֶׁנִּקְרָאוֹת מִצְוֹת הַמֶּלֶךְ שֶׁמְּקַבְּלִים כַּנַּ״ל.

שֶׁנִּקְרָאוֹת נֵר מִצְוָה אַף עַל פִּי שֶׁנִּקְרָאוֹת גַּם כֵּן מִצְוֹת

---

243. II Samuel 7:19.

244. Thus the radiance of the Torah manifests the inner "form" which constitutes the deep structure of the *sefirot*: the male "radiance" as opposed to the female "vessel." This inner form of the *sefirot* (and thus of all spirituality and all existence) is expressed by the Tetragrammaton.

245. I.e., the recipient, paralleling *malchut*, the recipient of the energy channeled through the nine *sefirot* to *yesod*, the emanator.

246. Ezekiel 1:28.

247. Numbers 12:6.

248. Hosea 12:11. "Images" here signifies dramatic metaphors and parables.

249. This phrase might suggest that the *mitzvah* relates to the supernal, male aspect, expressed by *Havaya*.

ifested in a variety of vessels,[250] and is [more generally] called the "lamp of the *mitzvah*." Nonetheless, [the lamp of the mitzvah] bears the imprinted image of the Glory of *Havaya* of *Atzilut* itself.[251] This is the theme of Adam, [as] "I will be in the image of the Supernal One,"[252] and as the verse, [that he was created] "in Our [G-d's] image."

This is what is meant by "and you shall bind [the *tefillin*] for a sign,"[253] thus including all the *mitzvot*, for [the Essence] is expressed by being vested in their actual performance.

This is how G-d is close to everyone equally, for they call upon Him "in truth," meaning with the truth of the inwardness of His Essence, as this is expressed in the 248 [Positive] *mitzvot*, relating to the 248 limbs, etc. The beginning is lodged specifically in the end.[254]

And the proof: the World to Come is gained only by actually performing *mitzvot* in the physical realm (and as was explained above,[255] that *the lamp of the mitzvah* is the vessel, in particular, which contains the light, the oil and the wick).[256]

---

250. I.e., the lamp of the mitzvah, including being associated with *Havaya*.

251. The Glory of G-d, *Havaya*, is the male form (*tzelem*); this imprints into *the lamp of the mitzvah*, the female image (*demut*).

252. EDAMEH L'EYLON. Earthly man, *adam*, has been created in the image of Supernal Man, *Adam Elyon*, referred to in the vision of the Prophet Ezekiel (1:26). Although the etymological origin of the word *adam* is *adamah*, earth, it may also be derived from the verb *damah*, "to be like," from which also the word *demut*, image, is derived. It is fittingly exemplified in the expression, in Isaiah 14:14, *edameh l'eylon*, "I will be like the One Above," as pointed out in *Shnei Luchot HaBrit*, mentioned below.

Terrestrial man consists of 248 organs, etc., through which the vitality of the organism is distributed, each organ receiving its appropriate power: the eye to see, and so forth. The li-

הוי"ה אֲבָל הוּא בָּא בְּכֵלִים מְכֵּלִים שׁוֹנִים וְנִקְרָא נֵר מִצְוָה כו' וְעִם כָּל זֶה הֲרֵי זֶה בִּדְמוּת כְּבוֹד הוי"ה דַּאֲצִילוּת עַצְמוֹ מַמָּשׁ שֶׁזֶּהוּ עִנְיַן אָדָם אֲדַמֶּה לְעֶלְיוֹן מַמָּשׁ וּכְמוֹ שֶׁכָּתוּב כִּדְמוּתֵינוּ כו'.

וְזֶהוּ וּקְשַׁרְתָּם לְאוֹת כו' שֶׁכּוֹלֵל כָּל הַמִּצְוֹת כו' שֶׁבָּא בְּדֶרֶךְ הִתְלַבְּשׁוּת מַמָּשׁ בְּסוֹף מַעֲשֶׂה כַּנַ"ל.

שֶׁבָּזֶה קָרוֹב ה' לַכֹּל בְּשָׁוֶה לְפִי שֶׁיִּקְרָאוּהוּ בֶאֱמֶת בַּאֲמִתַּת פְּנִימִית עַצְמוּתוֹ כְּמוֹ שֶׁהוּא דְּרמ"ח פִּקּוּדִין רמ"ח אֵבָרִים כו' וְנָעוּץ תְּחִלָּתָן בְּסוֹפָן דַּוְקָא.

וּרְאָיָה לָזֶה מִמַּה שֶׁהָעוֹלָם הַבָּא אֵינוֹ רַק מִמִּצְוֹת בְּפוֹעַל מַמָּשׁ בְּגַשְׁמִיּוּת דַּוְקָא (וְכַנַ"ל בְּפֵירוּשׁ נֵר מִצְוָה שֶׁהוּא הַמַּחֲזִיק הָאוֹר וְהַשֶּׁמֶן וְהַפְּתִילָה כו'):

---

ving soul is one and indivisible, but the vitality that flows from it is diffused in the organism in various degrees to provide just the right kind of power to each particular organ and limb. See Rabbi Menachem Azaria of Pano, *Asarah Maamarot,* Maamar *Eim Kol Chai*, part 2, ch. 33; *Shnei Luchot HaBrit* 3a, 20b, 268b, 301b. See also Talmud, *Yevamot* 61a.

253. Deuteronomy 6:8. The author continues expounding the Shema.

254. As explained at length above, *Atzmut,* G-d's Essence, is manifested in the actual performance of *mitzvot.*

255. Chapter 6, end.

256. Hence, just as the most important part of the lamp is the vessel, for it contains everything within it, so too it is most important to actually perform *mitzvot*, physically, for they specifically express G-d's Essence.

SUMMARY
OF CHAPTER SEVEN

Hence, *G-d is close to all who call upon Him, to all who call upon Him in truth.*

The truth of *Havaya*, the Essence, is close through being vested in Torah and *mitzvot.* In contrast to prayer—in which there are many different levels depending on the spiritual root of one's soul—G-d's *Essence* is vested in Torah and *mitzvot* and is close to everyone equally.

Hence the verse *Let us make Man in our Form and in our Image*: Through Torah one attains the Essential Form of *Havaya—z'a* of *Atzilut*, and through *mitzvot*, one attains the Divine Image—*malchut*, the recipient. Nonetheless, the Essential Form is engraved in the Image as well, for here too, He is close, for one calls upon Him in truth.

This also relates to the theme of a lamp, as in the verse *for the* mitzvah *is a lamp and the Torah is light.*

Indeed, it is specifically the *mitzvot*—in contrast to prayer—that cause one to reach contemplation of *yichuda ila'ah*, which in turn acts as oil with which one can consume any negative emotions (i.e. *dark radiance*) and also be divinely inspired (i.e. *illuminating radiance*).

INTRODUCTION TO CHAPTER EIGHT

This chapter introduces the theme of *teshuvah*, as a further spiritual dimension, which in some sense transcends the *mitzvot*.

Ethics of the Fathers states: "One hour of *teshuvah* and good deeds in this world is better than the whole life of the World to Come." Why is *teshuvah* mentioned before good deeds?

The answer is that exalted as the *mitzvot* are, *teshuvah* reaches an even higher level. Through *teshuvah*, the *mitzvot* themselves achieve a greater spiritual effect, eliciting the "Great Kindness" of the Divine.

Hence "Moshiach will influence the completely righteous in *teshuvah*." The righteous are perfect in their observance of the *mitzvot*, but through the additional dimension of *teshuvah* they achieve far more. Through *teshuvah*, the negative realm itself is induced to recognize G-d, which brings about the exaltation of the Divine.

Thus the question concerning the passage from Ethics of the Fathers is answered. The new focus on the transformation of the negative carries through into the following chapters.

8.
THE POWER OF TESHUVAH

Now, the Sages said: "One hour of *teshuvah* and good deeds in this world is better than the whole life of the World to Come."[257] Why is *teshuvah* mentioned before good deeds? Surely, since action is the main thing—as explained above, that "the beginning is lodged in the end"—why should *teshuvah* have to come first?

SUPERNAL GREAT KINDNESS

Although one definitely elicits [energy] from the truth of the radiance of the Essence of *Ein Sof* by performing Torah and *mitzvot*, there has to be a powerful flow from the supernal great kindness of the Essence to reveal what is particularly hidden in the Essence, where "thought cannot grasp Him at all."

Hence the verse, "His kindness is so powerful for us"[258]: the kindness of His Essence overpowers far greater than the set amount that flows through the *seder hishtalshelut* of the *kav* and *chut*.[259] This is so that it should be manifest below, vested [in Torah and *mitzvot*] so that "the truth of G-d is eternal"[260]—that the truth of the Essence of *Havaya* should be revealed in the terrestrial world as in the celestial world.

This tremendous force of great kindness is only manifest in the observance of Torah and *mitzvot* when it is preceded by *teshuvah*, which transforms the evil itself to good. This transcends Torah and *mitzvot*, for their purpose is merely to separate between good and evil.[261] Hence our Sages say[262] that *baalei teshuvah* are greater than the completely righteous, for those whose righteousness is defined by their observance of Torah and *mitzvot* cannot stand in the place where the *baalei teshuvah* stand.[263] Thus,

---

257. *Avot* 4:17.

258. Psalms 117:2.

259. See footnote 182.

260. Psalms ibid. The word "eternal" can also mean "for the world."

261. I.e., by performing Torah and *mitzvot*, one elevates *physical creation* to a G-dly stature, utilizing *it* for a G-dly purpose, thus separating "good—whatever utilized for G-d's service, from evil—that which cannot be made use of."

Teshuvah that results out of a tremendous

(ח)

וְהִנֵּה אָמְרוּ רַבּוֹתֵינוּ זִכְרוֹנָם לִבְרָכָה דִּיָּפָה שָׁעָה אַחַת בִּתְשׁוּבָה וּמַעֲשִׂים טוֹבִים בָּעוֹלָם הַזֶּה דַּוְקָא מִכָּל חַיֵּי הָעוֹלָם הַבָּא הֲרֵי הִזְכִּיר תְּשׁוּבָה קוֹדֶם לְמַעֲשִׂים טוֹבִים וּמֵאַחַר שֶׁהַמַּעֲשֶׂה עִיקָר מִטַּעַם הַנַּ״ל דְּנָעוּץ תְּחִלָּתָן בְּסוֹפָן דַּוְקָא לָמָּה צָרִיךְ לִתְשׁוּבָה קוֹדֶם כו׳.

אַךְ הִנֵּה אַף עַל פִּי שֶׁבְּוַדַּאי נִמְשָׁךְ מֵאֲמִתַּת אוֹר מַהוּתוֹ וְעַצְמוּתוֹ אֵין סוֹף בָּרוּךְ הוּא בְּתוֹרָה וּמִצְוֹת כַּנַּ״ל הֲרֵי צָרִיךְ לִהְיוֹת זֶה עַל יְדֵי הִתְגַּבְּרוּת גְּדוֹלָה מֵרַב חֶסֶד הָעֶלְיוֹן שֶׁבְּעַצְמוּת מַמָּשׁ שֶׁיִּהְיֶה בָּא בְּגִלּוּי כְּמוֹ שֶׁהוּא בְּהֶעְלֵם עַצְמוּתוֹ מַמָּשׁ דְּלֵית מַחֲשָׁבָה תְּפִיסָא בֵּיהּ כְּלָל כַּנַּ״ל.

וּכְמוֹ שֶׁכָּתוּב כִּי גָבַר עָלֵינוּ חַסְדּוֹ הָעַצְמִי בְּהִתְגַּבְּרוּת גְּדוֹלָה הַרְבֵּה יֶתֶר מִכְּפִי הַמִּדָּה הַקְּצוּבָה הַבָּא בְּסֵדֶר הִשְׁתַּלְשְׁלוּת דְּקַו וְחוּט כו׳ וְלָבֹא עַד לְמַטָּה מַמָּשׁ בְּדֶרֶךְ הִתְלַבְּשׁוּת עַל כָּל פָּנִים כַּנַּ״ל כְּדֵי לִהְיוֹת וֶאֱמֶת ה׳ לְעוֹלָם אֲמִתִּית הָעַצְמִיּוּת דַּהוי״ה יָבֹא לְגִלּוּי לְעוֹלָם לְמַטָּה כְּמוֹ לְמַעְלָה כו׳.

וְהִנֵּה בְּחִינַת הִתְגַּבְּרוּת רַב חֶסֶד זֶה אִי אֶפְשָׁר לָבֹא גַּם בְּתוֹרָה וּמִצְוֹת כִּי אִם עַל יְדֵי הַקְדָּמַת עִנְיַן הַתְּשׁוּבָה דַּוְקָא שֶׁהוּא הִיפּוּךְ הָרָע עַצְמוֹ לְטוֹב שֶׁזֶּה עוֹלֶה לְמַעְלָה מִתּוֹרָה וּמִצְוֹת שֶׁאֵינוֹ אֶלָּא לְהַבְדִּיל בֵּין טוֹב וָרָע כו׳ וּלְכַךְ אָמְרוּ דְּבַעֲלֵי תְשׁוּבָה גְּדוֹלִים מִצַּדִּיקִים גְּמוּרִים שֶׁצַּדִּיקִים גְּמוּרִים בְּתוֹרָה וּמִצְוֹת אֵינָם יְכוֹלִים לַעֲמוֹד בַּמָּקוֹם שֶׁבַּעֲלֵי תְשׁוּבָה

---

love for G-d however, actually transforms one's previous *negative* actions to good, for "inasmuch as his soul had been in a barren wilderness, and infinitely removed from the light of the Divine, his soul now thirsts for G-d even more than the souls of the righteous. Regarding such great love our Sages said: 'The *baal teshuvah's* premeditated sins become, in his case, like virtues, 'since he has thereby attained to this great love." (*Tanya*, ch. 7)

262. *Berachot* 34b.

263. TZADDIKIM and BAALEI TESHUVAH: The

"Moshiach will influence the completely righteous in *teshuvah*"[264] —to raise them higher.[265]

ELEVATING G-D'S GLORY—THROUGH QUELLING THE NEGATIVE

The reason [for the greater status of the *baalei teshuvah*] is as it says in the *Zohar*, that "when the *sitra achra*[266] is quelled, the glory of G-d rises."[267] [The Glory of G-d rises] despite the fact that the root of [the *sitra achra*] is only from the "rear" of the Name *Elokim*—its 48 latter combinations.[268] Thus the verse says "Praise G-d all nations," which expresses the nullification of total *yesh* from the *yesh* of *kelipat nogah*,[269] manifest in the Seventy Princes,[270] as in the future, when G-d "will turn towards the nations" [indicating their positive transformation].[271]

This, in essence, corresponds to *teshuvah*, for the evil itself will be transformed to good. Specifically then G-d will pour over us—the Jewish people—His essential "kindness," so that "the truth of G-d," meaning the truth of the inwardness of His essence manifested in Torah and *mitzvot*, becomes revealed below as it is above.

Thus "the truth of G-d" literally enters the world[272]: "the world"

---

sinner who has repented excels over the perfectly righteous man, who had never sinned, because the *baal teshuvah* had tasted temptation and is therefore more vulnerable to further temptation. He must therefore exert greater resistance to sin than the person who has never sinned, and his reward is proportionate to his effort (*Rambam, Hilchot Teshuvah* 7:4).

In *Likkutei Torah, Balak* 73a ff., Rabbi Schneur Zalman quotes two Talmudic sources, one Mishnaic and the other Amoraic, in support of the view that a *baal teshuvah* is on a higher level than the perfectly righteous. The Mishnaic source states: One hour of repentance and good deeds in this world is worth more than all the life of the world to come" (*Avot* 4:17). The later Talmudic source states: "In the place where *baalei teshuvah* stand, perfect *tzaddikim* cannot stand" (*Berachot* 34b).

Applying these categories to the soul, Rabbi Schneur Zalman declares that in its pristine state in the heavenly abode, before descent to earth, the soul is in the category of *tzaddik*, but after its descent to earth it attains the higher level of *baal teshuvah*. Herein, Rabbi Schneur Zalman points out, is the "true explanation" of the soul's descent for the purpose of ascent. See also footnote 261.

264. *Zohar* III:153b.

265. In Chasidut, the concept of *teshuvah* and *baal teshuvah* is not limited to actual transgression by commission or omission, and repentance thereof. That is only one aspect of a broader perspective of *teshuvah*, and, indeed, the lowest aspect of it. The Hebrew term for this form of *teshuvah* would be *charatah* ("repentance," or "penitence"). *Teshuvah*, on the other hand, means "return" and is not necessarily connected with sin. It is rather the constant striving of the soul to return to its Source in G-d, which is described in the *Zohar* (I:217b) as the "striving of the

עוֹמְדִים כו׳ וְזֶהוּ דְּמָשִׁיחַ אָתָא לַאֲתָבָא צַדִּיקִים גְּמוּרִים בִּתְשׁוּבָה לְהַעֲלוֹתָם יוֹתֵר.

מִטַּעַם שֶׁאָמַר בַּזֹּהַר דְּכַד אִתְכַּפְיָיא סִטְרָא אָחֳרָא אִסְתַּלַּק יְקָרָא דְקוּדְשָׁא בְּרִיךְ הוּא כו׳ אַף עַל פִּי שֶׁאֵין שָׁרְשָׁם רַק מֵאֲחוֹרַיִים דְּשֵׁם אֱלֹקִים בְּמ״ח צֵירוּפִים הָאַחֲרוֹנִים כו׳ וְזֶהוּ הַלְלוּ אֶת ה׳ כָּל גּוֹיִם כו׳ שֶׁהֵן בִּיטּוּל הַיֵּשׁ הַנִּפְרָד מִיֵּשׁ דִּקְלִיפַּת נוֹגַהּ בְּע׳ שָׂרִים כְּמוֹ שֶׁיִּהְיֶה לֶעָתִיד לָבֹא שֶׁיַּהֲפוֹךְ אֶל עַמִּים כו׳.

וְהוּא כְּמוֹ עִנְיַן הַתְּשׁוּבָה מַמָּשׁ שֶׁגַּם הָרַע עַצְמוֹ נֶהְפָּךְ לְטוֹב כו׳ אָז דַּוְקָא יִגְבַּר עָלֵינוּ כְּנֶסֶת יִשְׂרָאֵל חַסְדּוֹ הָעַצְמִית לִהְיוֹת אֱמֶת ה׳ אֲמִתִּית פְּנִימִית עַצְמוּתוֹ בְּתוֹרָה וּמִצְוֹת בָּא לִידֵי גִלּוּי לְמַטָּה כְּמוֹ לְמַעְלָה מַמָּשׁ.

שֶׁזֶּהוּ שֶׁכָּתוּב וֶאֱמֶת ה׳ לְעוֹלָם מַמָּשׁ וְהוּא הָעוֹלָם הַבָּא

---

soul to be absorbed into the Essence of the King."

In light of this concept of *teshuvah* it is clear why this experience is available to the soul only in the terrestrial world even if it goes through life on earth without a blemish. For in the terrestrial world the Divine Light is obscured and concealed behind the physical and material shells of things, and by the very nature of the physical world in which we live. At the same time, the soul itself is inhibited by its confinement in a physical body. As a result, the soul's natural striving to merge with G-d is greatly intensified by the very obstacles in its way. It is, by way of example, like a stream whose flow is hampered by cataracts, where the pressure of the flow is greatly increased by the very barriers in its way, making it gush and rush forward with greater force when the barrier is overcome.

266. SITRA ACHRA: Lit., "the other side," i.e. not the side of holiness; another term for evil in that it negates G-dliness. Anything that tends to separate from G-d belongs in the *sitra achra*, the root of evil. See also footnote 35.

267. *Zohar* II:128b.

268. The 5 letters of the Divine Name *Elokim* have 120 combinations. 72 of these are sacred, but the remaining 48 give sustenance to the negative realms. See *Torah Or* 109d. Although the negative realm is so low, it has great power to exalt G-d by being transformed.

269. See footnote 35.

270. Through which the 70 Nations of the world receive sustenance.

271. Hence the nations are not proper *yesh*, which would be totally negative, but are in the category of *nogah*, which contains goodness. In the future, this goodness will be exposed as the nations will be positively transformed.

272. See note 260.

refers to the World to Come, i.e., when the truth of G-d will "come" into the terrestrial world,[273] as the verse, "and it will be said on that day, behold this is our G-d—actually."[274]

Thus "*teshuvah*" is stated before "*good deeds*," in this world, for [although] it is on account of the *mitzvot*—the good deeds—that one merits the reward of the life of the World to Come, but without *teshuvah* the good deeds do not have any effect, for they are simply vessels for the indwelling of His Divine Essence.[275]

273. I.e., when Moshiach will come.

274. Isaiah 25:9.

שֶׁיָּבֹא אֱמֶת ה׳ לָעוֹלָם הַזֶּה כְּמוֹ שֶׁאָמַר וְאָמַר בַּיּוֹם הַהוּא הִנֵּה אֱלֹקֵינוּ זֶה מַמָּשׁ כו׳.

וְזֶהוּ שֶׁהִקְדִּים תְּשׁוּבָה לְמַעֲשִׂים טוֹבִים בָּעוֹלָם הַזֶּה דְּעַל יְדֵי זֶה יָבֹא שְׂכַר חַיֵּי הָעוֹלָם הַבָּא מִן הַמִּצְוֹת שֶׁהֵן מַעֲשִׂים טוֹבִים וּבְלֹא תְּשׁוּבָה אֵין הַמַּעֲשִׂים טוֹבִים מוֹעִילִים שֶׁאֵינָן רַק בְּחִינַת כֵּלִים לְבָד לְהַשְׁרָאַת עַצְמוּתוֹ יִתְבָּרֵךְ וְדַי לַמֵּבִין:

275. And *teshuvah* is the actual Divine Essence to fill the vessels of the *mitzvot*. So without *teshuvah* one lacks the most fundamental dimension.

SUMMARY
OF CHAPTER EIGHT

Having established that *mitzvot* are rooted in the most sublime source, and it is specifically they that enable one to attain spiritual oil and elicit G-d's Essence, the author now poses a question from a *Mishna* in *Avot* that states that there exists a further spiritual dimension, which in some sense transcends the *mitzvot*: *"One hour of teshuvah and good deeds in this world is better than the whole life of the World to Come."* Why is *teshuvah* mentioned before good deeds?

The author explains that for the radiance of G-d's Essence to flow into mitzvot, one must first perform *teshuvah*, which draws a tremendous force of great supernal kindness into the observance of Torah and *mitzvot.*

Hence *Moshiach will influence the completely righteous in* teshuvah. When the *sitra achra* is quelled through *teshuvah*, a greater radiance is elicited than that which is elicited through Torah observance. For while Torah observance differentiates between good and evil, *teshuvah* actually transforms evil into good.

Thus, *Praise G-d all nations*: The fact that the nations praise G-d is a *teshuvah* of sorts. Their praise causes *His* Essential *kindness to be mighty over us* (*Knesset Yisrael*), i.e., so that the truth of His Essence will be revealed in this terrestrial world through our deeds. Hence *teshuvah* precedes good deeds.

INTRODUCTION TO CHAPTER NINE

Returning to the image of the lamp, the discussion now concerns the relationship of the wick, signifying the body and the animal soul, to the spiritual quality of the oil, which expresses *chochmah* and selflessness.

The wick belongs to the realm of the negative, *Kelipat Nogah* (intermediary "shell"), which in itself conceals G-dliness yet at the same time possesses an extremely exalted spiritual source. For that which is highest falls lowest.

Therefore, in a sense, the wick is higher than the oil.

Following the same logic, when considering the two kinds of flame, the dark flame has a higher spiritual quality than the bright flame. In fact the brightness of the bright flame derives from the dark flame, meaning that the higher spiritual attainments of the person are the product of the struggle to transform one's evil desire.

Now the focus switches back to the oil, which includes within it the properties of both the dark and the bright flame.

Oil represents supernal *chochmah* as well as selflessness. There are two levels of selflessness: the first is the lower level of submission before the Divine, through which the wick is worn away. This is expressed by the dark flame, representing *teshuvah* and the transformation of the evil qualities in one's heart. The second level is described in the next chapter.

9.
CHAPTER NINE: OIL, WICK AND RADIANCE

Now we can understand the concept of the oil of the lamp, which conceals within it the two kinds of light: the bright radiance and the dark radiance, [which are revealed] when it is drawn into the wick, as explained above.

OIL AND WICK

First we have to consider why the oil specifically has to be drawn after the wick in order for the flame to join with the wick. Why should the oil, which is superior, be drawn specifically after the wick? Why is it that the flame burns only when there is a wick, and not simply from the oil itself? This must indicate that there is superiority in the wick over the oil, to the extent that the oil is no more than an intermediary joining the flame to the wick.

ROOTS

[It was explained earlier that the wick represents the body.] The root of the natural soul, the body, is far more sublime than the [divine] soul, for the natural soul stems from *kelipot* of *nogah*[276] which fell in the breaking of the vessels of the "seven kings" of *Tohu.*[277] As the

---

276. See above footnote 35. The source of the *kelipot*, including *nogah*, is the "breaking of the vessels," described in the next footnote.

277. SHEVIRAT HAKEILIM: The "breaking of the vessels," was a process whereby the intense Divine Light was substantially shut off, so to speak, and only "sparks" thereof fell from the upper realm into lower depths. By a further process of infinite reductions and contractions (*tzimtzum*), the Divine emanations eventually materialized into Four Worlds. See elaboration in footnote 279.

The idea of *shevirat hakeilim*, at any rate the idea of the existence of primordial worlds before our own cosmos came into being, is not original in Lurianic Kabbalah, nor in the *Zohar*, from which the idea was developed. Its origin can be traced to a much older *Midrash*, (*Bereishit Rabbah* 3:9) where Rabbi Avahu deduces from the verse, "And G-d saw the light that it was good," (Genesis 1:4) that prior to creating the present "good" world, G-d "had created worlds and destroyed them, saying, 'this [world] pleases Me; the others did not.'"

A similar idea is expressed in another *Midrash* (*Bereishit Rabbah*, end of ch. 12; *Pesikta Rabbati* 40), in explanation of the fact that the Creation narrative begins with the repeated use of the Divine Name *Elokim*, but later introduces also the so-called Tetragramaton, *Havaya*. Declares the *Midrash*: At first G-d created the world in the attribute of stern justice, *din*, (as denoted by the Divine Name *Elokim*). But seeing that it could not exist under the rule of stern justice alone, He combined it with the attribute of mercy, *rachamim*, (as denoted by the name *Havaya*). By way of il-

(ט)

וּבְכָל זֶה יוּבַן עִנְיַן הַשֶּׁמֶן שֶׁבְּנֵר שֶׁיֵּשׁ בּוֹ בְּהֶעְלֵם ב׳ גַּוְונֵי אוֹר דִּנְהוֹרָא חִוְורָא וְנְהוֹרָא אוּכָּמָא כַּנַ״ל כַּאֲשֶׁר נִשְׁאָב וְנִמְשָׁךְ אַחַר הַפְּתִילָה וְהָאוֹר כַּנַ״ל.

דְּהִנֵּה יֵשׁ לְהָבִין תְּחִילָּה מַה שֶּׁצָּרִיךְ שֶׁיִּהְיֶה הַשֶּׁמֶן נִמְשָׁךְ אַחַר הַפְּתִילָה דַּוְקָא כְּדֵי שֶׁיִּהְיֶה חִיבּוּר הָאוֹר בַּפְּתִילָה וְאֵיךְ הַשֶּׁמֶן שֶׁהוּא גָּבוֹהַּ יוּמְשַׁךְ אַחַר הַפְּתִילָה וְאֵין הָאוֹר דּוֹלֵק רַק בַּפְּתִילָה וְלֹא בְּשֶׁמֶן מִזֶּה מוּכְרָח שֶׁיֵּשׁ מַעֲלָה יְתֵירָה בַּפְּתִילָה יוֹתֵר מִן הַשֶּׁמֶן עַד שֶׁהַשֶּׁמֶן אֵינוֹ אֶלָּא אֶמְצָעִי לְחַבֵּר הָאוֹר בַּפְּתִילָה.

הָעִנְיָן הוּא כַּיָּדוּעַ שֶׁיֵּשׁ שֹׁרֶשׁ לְנֶפֶשׁ הַטִּבְעִית שֶׁהוּא הַגּוּף לְמַעְלָה הַרְבֵּה מִן הַנְּשָׁמָה לְפִי שֶׁנֶּפֶשׁ הַטִּבְעִית נִלְקְחָה מִקְּלִיפַּת נוֹגַהּ שֶׁנָּפְלוּ בִּשְׁבִירַת הַכֵּלִים מִז׳

---

lustration the *Midrash* offers the following parable: A king had some empty precious glasses. Said the king, "If I pour hot water into them, they will shatter; if I pour cold water into them, they will crack." So he mixed the hot with the cold and poured the tepid water into the glasses and they remained whole. Similarly the Holy One, blessed be He, said, "If I create the world by Mercy alone, sin would abound; if by strict Justice alone, it could not endure. I will create Justice tempered with Mercy, and would that it exist."

The *Zohar* (I:24b), referring to the said Midrashim, cryptically identifies the primordial world as the world of *Tohu*. (It also notes that the 2nd, 3rd and 4th words of Genesis 2:4, תולדות השמים וארץ, contain the acronym.) Elsewhere, the *Zohar* (III:128a; 135a ff; 142a ff.) sees in the apparently meaningless narrative about the kings of Edom, of whom nothing is stated except that each built a town and died (Gen. 36:31-39), an allusion to the primordial forces of sternness, *gevurah*, which could not exist without the ameliorating quality of *chesed*, compassion. Hence they were withdrawn and substituted by more manageable, as it were, forces of synthesized Divine attributes, of stern justice tempered by compassion, and vice versa.

In Lurianic Kabbalah (*Eitz Chayim* ch. 9 and elsewhere) the cosmogonic process is described in terms of *Shevirat hakelim* and is intimately linked with the doctrine of *Tzimtzum*, referred to earlier (fn. 110).

These "fallen sparks" of the Divine *sefirot* in *Tohu*—whose character is described as "abundance of light and paucity of vessels"—are preserved in the realms of *kelipah.*

verse states, "these are the kings [which ruled in the land of Edom] before there was a king of the children of Israel."[278] The radiance of *Tohu*[279] [the kings of Edom] preceded the realm of *Tikkun* [the kings of Israel, expressed by] the Divine Name [whose numerical value is] forty-five מ"ה of Adam.[280]

Hence there is root for the creatures and animals—the face of the lion and the face of the ox of the Chariot[281]—higher than that of

---

Hence the *maamar* can state that the source of the natural soul, *Kelipat Nogah* of *Tohu*, transcends that of the Divine Soul, the *sefirot* of *Tikkun*.

278. Genesis 36:31.

279. TOHU AND TIKKUN: Creation is conceived in Kabbalah and Chasidut in terms of *Giluy Or Ein Sof*, "revelation of the Infinite Light." Together with the metaphor of light, and inseparable from it, is that of *kelim*, "vessels," or "instruments." Light *per se* is invisible; it becomes perceptible only in conjunction with something that reflects the light; i.e. a *keli*, "vessel." Thus, "lights" and "vessels" (*orot v'kelim*) are as inseparable as matter and form. In either case, one is inconceivable without the other. For example, the power of vision is *or*, the eye is the *keli*; the mind is *or*, the brain is *keli*; the idea is *or*, the words conveying it are the *kelim*.

The "light" and the "vessel" must obviously be compatible. The container must fit the contents; no container could contain anything beyond its capacity. If the glare of the light is too strong for the eye, the eye will be "blinded"—it will not see anything and simply will not function. A teacher who wishes to convey an idea (*or*) to a pupil must reduce it to the pupil's mental grasp (*keli*). Otherwise the student would only get confused. Where the capacity of the vessel is overtaxed, the vessel must break, and the contents spilled or scattered.

An analogy: A word consists of two or more letters. When the letters are joined together in the proper order into a word, they form a "vessel" for a concept. If you break up the word into separate letters, the concept vanishes. Now, in the world of *Tohu*, the Divine emanations come forth as separate, distinct and disjointed letters, as it were, each radiating an intense light from its Source in the *Ein Sof*. But in that state the letters cannot form words, or ideas; they are unproductive. The strong, inexorable individuality of the letters has to be reduced, so that they can be put together into word patterns, reflecting their original archetypes though in a reduced intensity.

The Divine attributes—*sefirot*—in their original pristine state, as they emanate from the *Ein Sof*, are absolute, distinct, and mutually exclusive. In this state, *chesed* has no relation to *gevurah*; they are two opposites and incompatible, like fire and water. This early phase of Divine emanation produced the world of *Tohu*. Here the Divine *sefirot* are at the height of their intensity, each one a separate potency, unqualified and unmitigated.

Inasmuch as the *sefirot* are conceived under two aspects, namely *or* (light) and *keli* (vessel), standing in relation to each other as form to matter, the character of the Divine *sefirot* in *Tohu* is described in terms of "abundance of light and paucity of vessels." In other words, the light was too intense to be controlled or contained. This led to *Shevirat hakelim*, the "breaking of the vessels," a process whereby the intense Divine Light was substantially shut off, as it were, and only "sparks" thereof fell from the upper realm into lower depths.

Thus, the "breaking of the vessels" gave rise to a new, orderly world, called, the World of *Tikkun*, the "repaired" or "restored" world. *Tohu* is described as "abundance of light and a paucity of vessels," and *Tikkun* is described in the reverse, "paucity of light and abundance of vessels."

In *Tikkun* the Divine *sefirot* are integrated

מְלָכִים דְּתֹהוּ דִּכְתִיב וְאֵלֶּה הַמְּלָכִים כו' לִפְנֵי מְלוֹךְ מֶלֶךְ לִבְנֵי יִשְׂרָאֵל כו' דִּבְחִינַת אוֹרוֹת דְּתֹהוּ קָדְמוּ לִבְחִינַת הַתִּיקּוּן דְּשֵׁם מָ"ה דְּאָדָם.

וְעַל כֵּן יֵשׁ שֹׁרֶשׁ לְחַיּוֹת וּבְהֵמוֹת דִּפְנֵי אַרְיֵה וּפְנֵי שׁוֹר דְּמֶרְכָּבָה לְמַעְלָה מִבְּחִינַת אָדָם וְעַל כֵּן נוֹשְׂאוֹת אֶת

---

and intertwined. The ten *sefirot* can now be classified into two major patterns, *sechel* (intellect) and *middot* (emotions), the former influencing the latter. Under the control of *sechel* the *middot* are ameliorated. No longer can each *middah* be absolute—unlimited *chesed*, or unlimited *gevurah*, but we get *chesed* in *gevurah* and vice versa. The ten Divine *sefirot* now manifest themselves in conglomerate *partzufim* (lit. "faces"), wherein each *sefirah* is composed of ten *sefirot*, and each *sefirah* is in itself a complete entity in terms of the Four Worlds, and all *sefirot* form a complete image, or "face."

280. The four letters of the name *Havaya* may be "spelled" in four different ways. Each spelling yields a different numerical value (—see footnote 131). The numerical value of *Havaya* when spelled out thus יו"ד ה"א וא"ו ה"א is 45 or מ"ה. The numerical value of the word *adam*, man, is also 45.

The Divine Name מ"ה causes the integration of the *sefirot*, for this Name connotes *bittul* (self-nullification) as in the verse (Exodus 16:7), "and we are 'what.'" Thus, regarding the *sefirot*, this allows for a state of intergraded unity known as the world of *Tikkun*. *Tikkun* is the source of the divine soul in man.

When spelled out thus יו"ד ה"ה ו"ו ה"ה, the numerical value of *Havaya* would be 52 or ב"ן, the numerical value of the word *behemah*, animal, the source of the animal soul.

In order to complete the *Tikkun*, the divine name מ"ה must sift through and rescue the sparks of *Tohu* which are concealed in the Divine Name ב"ן. In human terms, this refers to the G-dly soul's descent and refinement of the animal soul. For man's mission is to elicit increased Divine Light into the world, the "vessels." Man is to elevate the fallen sparks, by utilizing the material world for Divine purpose (performance of *mitzvot*, etc.) rather than indulgence, and by rejecting what G-d has forbidden him. (See *Likkutei Torah*, *Re'eh* 27c)

281. MERKAVAH: Ezekiel (ch. 1) tells of his vision of the Divine Chariot and Throne:

"I saw there was a storm-wind coming from the north, a great cloud and a blazing fire, and from its midst like the pure luminescence from the midst of fire. And from its midst [I saw] the image of four *chayot* (angelic creatures)...And the image of the faces was: The face of a man, and the face of a lion on its right...and the face of an ox on the left...and the face of an eagle...And the complexion of the *chayot*—their appearance was like fiery coals...The *chayot* ran and returned as the appearance of a flash of lightning.

"As I observed the *chayot*, I saw one *ofan* (angelic being) on the floor [of the firmament] at the side of each of the *chayot*...The appearance of the *ofanim* and their work was like chrysolite...when the *chayot* moved, the *ofanim* moved beside them, and when the *chayot* raised themselves from the ground, the *ofanim* raised themselves...Above the firmament which is over their heads was the likeness of a throne, in appearance like sapphire, and upon the likeness of the throne was a likeness with the appearance of a man [as it were] upon it above...This was the appearance of the likeness of the glory of the L-rd..."

It is known that every physical creation must have a celestial source, from which it receives its life-force and existence. Its very being and physical characteristics are synonymous to their spiritual source, albeit

Man. And thus they "carry the throne" [on which there is the form of a man]. Similarly, in their descent [into this physical world], man is sustained by eating animals and vegetables,[282] strengthening the power of his mind [man's superior quality]. Similarly, more sublime, regarding the animal offerings the verse states,[283] "the food of My fire, a pleasant savor for *Havaya*"—of *Tikkun*. [But on a human level,] "Man lives by bread"[284] and cannot exist without it, but the vegetable and animal world *can* exist without man. This is because the root of the vegetable and animal worlds is higher than that of man.[285]

THE WICK'S VALUE

Hence, it is the consumption of the wick—corresponding to the body—which is the main factor in eliciting the supernal [bright] radiance to illuminate the soul from the aforementioned second level of *sovev kol almin*.[286] Thus the verse states, "For You, G-d, are my lamp," meaning, that although the oil causes the radiance to be joined to the wick, it is actually only an intermediary. Because the primary cause for the radiance is the consumption of the wick, and the oil only causes the flame cleave to it.

In addition, the fact that the oil is drawn into the wick and is consumed, flowing into the flame, is also on account of the wick. Thus the oil is drawn specifically to the wick. The oil has the quality of *chochmah* [287] of Torah and *mitzvot*, and the root of the

---

physical. All living creatures are derived from the spiritual angels that are found in the Divine Chariot and consequently, the faces of the lion and the ox in the Divine Chariot are the sources for all physical animals and beasts. Moreover, the *chayot* which have the faces of a lion and an ox are the aspect of *gevurah*, as it is written in Ezekiel 1:13 "burning like the appearance of torches," and the angels known as *seraphim* derive their name from "coals of fire." Thus, physical animals that evolve from these angels are strong and powerful, and their flesh is red, the color of "anger" or "severity" (*Likkutei Torah*, *B'ha'alotcha* 31c-d).

All the beasts derive their energy from the face of the lion, all the animals from the face of the ox and all the birds from the face of the eagle (*Torah Or* 41b).

The two souls of every Jew, G-dly soul and the animal soul, are also rooted in the Chariot. However, the G-dly soul's source is known as "Adam," man, as it is written in Genesis (1:27), "And G-d created man in His image," and in Ezekiel 1:26 it is written, "upon the likeness of the throne a likeness with the appearance of a man." In creation of G-dly soul and its descent to this world, the light found within the *Sefirot*—the origin of man—descends to this world, passing through the chariot and specifically its human face, which is thus considered a more proximate source of G-dly soul.

The animal soul is rooted not in the *Sefirot* but in the chariot. It then descends to a lowly derivative (dregs) of the *ofanim*, which are of a lower order than the *chayot*. The animal soul is derived from the "dregs" of the *ofanim*, but is

הַכִּסֵּא כו׳ וּכְמוֹ לְמַטָּה מַטָּה בִּירִידָתָן עוֹד הָאָדָם נִיזּוֹן מִן הַחַי וְצוֹמֵחַ וְיִתְחַזֵּק כֹּחַ שִׂכְלוֹ כו׳ וְכַךְ לְמַעְלָה נֶאֱמַר בְּקָרְבָּן בְּהֵמָה לַחְמִי לְאִשַּׁי רֵיחַ נִיחוֹחַ לַהוי״ה דְּתִיקּוּן וּכְמוֹ שֶׁכָּתוּב בְּמָקוֹם אַחֵר כְּמוֹ שֶׁעַל הַלֶּחֶם יִחְיֶה הָאָדָם וְלֹא יִתְקַיֵּים בִּלְעָדוֹ וְהַצּוֹמֵחַ וְחַי יִתְקַיְּימוּ בְּלֹא אָדָם לְפִי שֶׁשֹּׁרֶשׁ הַצּוֹמֵחַ וְחַי בְּשָׁרְשׁוֹ גָּבוֹהַּ מִשֹּׁרֶשׁ הָאָדָם.

וְעַל כֵּן עַל יְדֵי כִלְיוֹן הַפְּתִילָה שֶׁהוּא הַגּוּף הוּא עִיקַּר הַגּוֹרֵם הַמְשָׁכַת הָאוֹר הָעֶלְיוֹן לְהָאִיר אֶת הַנְּשָׁמָה מִבְּחִינַת סוֹבֵב כָּל עָלְמִין הַכְּלָלִי הַנַּ״ל שֶׁזֶּהוּ שֶׁכָּתוּב כִּי אַתָּה נֵרִי הוי״ה כו׳ כִּי הֲגַם שֶׁהַשֶּׁמֶן הוּא הַסִּיבָּה לְחִיבּוּר הָאוֹר בַּפְּתִילָה כַּנַּ״ל הֲרֵי זֶה רַק מְמוּצָּע אֲבָל עִיקַּר הַסִּיבָּה הוּא כִלְיוֹן הַפְּתִילָה דַּוְקָא רַק שֶׁעַל יְדֵי הַשֶּׁמֶן הוּא סִיבָּה שֶׁיֵּאָחֵז בּוֹ הָאוֹר.

וְגַם מַה שֶּׁהַשֶּׁמֶן נִשְׁאָב בַּפְּתִילָה וְנִכְלֶה וְנִמְשָׁךְ וְנִשְׁאָב בָּאוֹר גַּם הוּא עַל יְדֵי הַפְּתִילָה וְהוּא הַטַּעַם שֶׁהַשֶּׁמֶן נִמְשָׁךְ אַחַר הַפְּתִילָה דַּוְקָא לִיכָּלֵל בָּאוֹר כו׳ לְפִי שֶׁהַשֶּׁמֶן הוּא בִּבְחִינַת חָכְמָה דְּתוֹרָה וּמִצְוֹת כַּנַּ״ל וְשֹׁרֶשׁ

---

originally rooted in the face of the ox of the Divine Chariot. (*Likkutei Torah*, *Vayikra* 2b)

In addition to all physical living creatures finding their source in the Chariot, the "negative forces" are rooted in the "storm-wind...a great cloud and a blazing fire" amid which Ezekiel beheld his vision. These forces refer to the three totally impure *kelipot*, which contain absolutely no good, and are the source of any thought, speech or action by mankind in transgression of a negative command in the Torah (*Tanya* ch. 1; ch. 6; *Likkutei Torah*, *Chukat* 60a).

282. Because their source is higher than man, they can sustain him.

283. Numbers 28:2 and 8.

284. See Deuteronomy 8:3.

285. See *Iggeret Hakodesh*, end of section 20, and *Kuntres Achron*, section 5, p. 157a.

286. The body has a more transcendent source than the soul. Thus, when one trains oneself and transforms one's bodily desires to spiritual desires, one elicits are more supernal revelation than that which is capable of radiating by result of the soul alone.

287. OIL AND CHOCHMAH: See Menachot 85b: "Tekoa was the leading city in Israel for oil [the oil for use in the Beit Hamikdash was brought from there]. Joab brought a wise woman from Tekoa (II Samuel 14:2). Why from Tekoa? Rabbi Yochanan said: Since they

wick—corresponding to the natural soul, is far more sublime than [the Divine Name] מ"ה of *chochmah* of *Tikkun*. [Hence the wick has the power to draw the oil.[288]]

The proof for this is from the theme of "one moment of *teshuvah* and good deeds" discussed earlier.[289] *Teshuvah* transforms the evil itself to good, and specifically intensifies the great force of G-d's Kindness to us, bringing the "Truth of G-d to the world," i.e., the World *to Come*, the reward resulting from observance of the Torah and *mitzvot*.

Thus, in the Shema, following the verse, "and you shall love G-d, with all your heart"—with both your good and evil inclinations, "and with all your soul[290]"—expressing the consumption of the wick, we then recite the verse, "these words which I command you," thus revealing the most exalted radiance, the most sublime level of *sovev kol almin* vested in the Torah and *mitzvot*.

OIL AS CHOCHMAH OF TORAH

Thus, the dark radiance which consumes the wick actually causes the revelation of the bright radiance from its source in the Essence of *Ein Sof* blessed be He, as the verse, "for You [G-d's Essence] illuminate my lamp."

Nonetheless, these two colors of light are revealed at the wick are the result of the oil, which causes the light to join the wick in these two colors. Without oil, the wick would swiftly be completely consumed, or the flame would immediately dart away.[291]

Similarly in the spiritual realms: "Oil" refers to the concealment of the radiance of Supernal *chochmah*[292] which is vested in Torah

---

were accustomed to [partaking of] oil, they were wise." Olive oil opens the heart—Rashi.

In Kabblistic terms: Oil, like *chochmah*, is hidden, for the nature of *chochmah* is to flow into even the lowest levels. Proof for this can be found in science books, that one can extract oil from everything, even from a stone, as the verse (Deuteronomy 32:13) states, "oil from a flint stone." For oil refers to the inner quality of everything, as *Pardes* explains, and as the verse states, "You have made them all with *chochmah*," that all created things contain the quality of *chochmah*, for *chochmah* is the inwardness and most vital of everythings. It is for this reason that the Torah's *chochmah* can be vested in, and relate to, even the lowest subjects. (*Maamarei Admur Hazaken*, 5568, vol. 2, p. 647) See also *Shaar HaYichud v'HaEmunah*, chapter 9.

288. Here too, the seemingly lower is of a higher source.

289. Chapter 8, beginning.

290. Apparently the vital soul.

הַפְּתִילָה שֶׁהוּא הַנֶּפֶשׁ הַטִּבְעִית הוּא לְמַעְלָה מַּעְלָה מִבְּחִינַת מָ"ה דְחָכְמָה דְתִקּוּן כַּנַ"ל.

וּרְאָיָה לָזֶה מֵעִנְיָן הַנַ"ל בְּשָׁעָה אַחַת בִּתְשׁוּבָה וּמַעֲשִׂים טוֹבִים שֶׁעַל יְדֵי תְשׁוּבָה דַּוְקָא שֶׁהוּא הִיפּוּךְ הָרָע עַצְמוֹ לְטוֹב עַל יְדֵי זֶה דַּוְקָא יִגְבַּר חַסְדּוֹ עָלֵינוּ לִהְיוֹת אֱמֶת ה' לְעוֹלָם שֶׁהוּא הָעוֹלָם הַבָּא שֶׁבָּא מִן הַתּוֹרָה וּמִצְוֹת כַּנַ"ל וְדַי לַמֵּבִין.

וְזֶהוּ שֶׁאַחַר וְאָהַבְתָּ בְּכָל לְבָבְךָ בִּשְׁנֵי יְצָרֶיךָ וּבְכָל נַפְשְׁךָ כו' שֶׁזֶּהוּ כִלְיוֹן הַפְּתִילָה הוּא שֶׁאָמַר אַחַר זֶה וְהָיוּ הַדְּבָרִים כו' אֲשֶׁר אָנֹכִי מְצַוְּךָ כו' שֶׁמִּתְגַּלֶּה עַל יְדֵי זֶה מִבְּחִינַת אוֹר הָעֶלְיוֹן בְּיוֹתֵר שֶׁהוּא סוֹבֵב הַכְּלָלִי שֶׁמְּלוּבָּשׁ בְּתוֹרָה וּמִצְוֹת כַּנַ"ל וְדַי לַמֵּבִין.

וְנִמְצָא שֶׁבְּחִינַת נְהוֹרָא אוּכְמָא הַשּׂוֹרֵף וּמְכַלֶּה לַפְּתִילָה עַל יְדֵי זֶה גּוֹרֵם מִמֵּילָא גִּלּוּי הָאוֹר הָעֶלְיוֹן דִּנְהוֹרָא חִוְּורָא מִמְּקוֹרוֹ שֶׁהוּא בְּעַצְמוּת אֵין סוֹף בָּרוּךְ הוּא כְּמוֹ שֶׁכָּתוּב כִּי אַתָּה תָּאִיר נֵרִי כו'.

אַךְ הִנֵּה עִם כָּל זֶה ב' גַּוְונֵי אוֹר הַלָּלוּ שֶׁמִּתְגַּלִּים בַּפְּתִילָה הוּא עַל יְדֵי הַשֶּׁמֶן שֶׁהוּא הַסִּיבָּה לְחִיבּוּר הָאוֹר בַּפְּתִילָה בְּב' גַּוָונִין הַלָּלוּ שֶׁהֲרֵי בְּלֹא שֶׁמֶן הָיָה הַפְּתִילָה כָּלָה וְנִשְׂרֶפֶת לְגַמְרֵי בִּמְהֵרָה אוֹ שֶׁהָיָה הָאוֹר קוֹפֵץ מֵעָלֶיהָ מִיָּד כַּנַ"ל.

וְכָךְ יוּבַן לְמַעְלָה דְהִנֵּה עִנְיַן הַשֶּׁמֶן הוּא בְּחִינַת הֶעְלֵם

291. See footnote 17.

292. CHOCHMAH ILA'AH – CHOCHMAH TATA'AH. There are two primary aspects of *chochmah*. *Chochmah ila'ah* (the higher *chochmah*) is *chochmah* within itself—i.e., receiving and being illuminated by the Infinite Light of *Or Ein Sof*. Regarding this Rabbi Schneur Zalman states in Tanya (note, ch. 35): "The light of the blessed *Ein Sof* does not become unified even in the world of *Atzilut*, unless it clothes itself first in the *sefirah* of *chochmah*—the reason being that the blessed *Ein Sof* is the true One Who is One Alone and apart from Whom there is nothing, and this is the level of *chochmah*." This aspect of *chochmah* is the *chochmah* of Torah, which would have been pertinent even if the worlds had not been created.

Chochmah tata'ah, (the lower *chochmah*) is *chochmah* outside of itself, i.e., as it flows downward to permeate and enliven the other *sefirot*. This aspect of *chochmah* is the *chochmah* of creation, and therefore would not exist had the worlds not been created (*Sefer HaLikkutim*, *Chochmah*, ch. 36).

and *mitzvot*. It is unable to enter the world by way of *hishtalshlut* [due to its transcendent loftiness], and can only enter the world by being vested [in Torah and *mitzvot*], as the verse states, "He wears radiance like a robe,"[293] which refers to the radiance of Torah.

THE NATURE OF TORAH

The Torah is called, "Primordial metaphor,"[294] and as the saying, "the outflowings of Supernal *chochmah*[295] are Torah"[296]: This indicates the tremendous descent of Supernal *chochmah*—"whose understanding is beyond reckoning"[297]—to be vested in physical matters, in laws and rules of the Written Torah and the Oral Torah, in the 248 Positive *mitzvot* and 365 Negative *mitzvot*.[298]

This corresponds to the nature of oil, which seeps down and is absorbed by whatever it contacts. Hence the oil seeps into the wick, to join it with the flame.

CHOCHMAH LEVEL ONE

[The two categories of flame] correspond to the two levels of *chochmah*: The first is the abnegation of the self before the Divine *Ayin*. This means arousing—even in physical terms—thoughts of *teshuvah* with tremendous subjugation and a contrite heart. This consumes the wick in the dark flame, which is expressed by crying out and elevation in prayer, pouring out one's soul and transforming the evil qualities of one's heart. This is caused by the oil that is drawn to the wick.[299]

---

293. Psalms 104:2.

294. Rashi on I Samuel 24:14. See *Torah Or* 42b.

295. Thus, deriving from, but not Supernal *chochmah* as it is itself.

296. *Bereishit Rabbah* 17:5, 44:17.

דְּאוֹר חָכְמָה עִלָּאָה שֶׁמְּלוּבָּשׁ בְּתוֹרָה וּמִצְוֹת שֶׁאִי אֶפְשָׁר לָבֹא בְּדֶרֶךְ הִשְׁתַּלְשְׁלוּת כְּלָל כִּי אִם דֶּרֶךְ הִתְלַבְּשׁוּת וּכְמוֹ עוֹטֶה אוֹר כַּשַּׂלְמָה שֶׁהוּא אוֹר דְּתוֹרָה.

וְנִקְרָא מְשַׁל הַקַּדְמוֹנִי וְכַמַּאֲמָר נוֹבְלוֹת חָכְמָה שֶׁל מַעְלָה תּוֹרָה כו' שֶׁזֶּהוּ עִנְיַן עוֹצֶם יְרִידָה וְהִתְלַבְּשׁוּת דְּחָכְמָה עִלָּאָה הָעַצְמִית שֶׁלִּתְבוּנָתוֹ אֵין מִסְפָּר כְּלָל בְּעִנְיָנִים גַּשְׁמִיִּים בַּהֲלָכוֹת וְדִינִין דְּתוֹרָה שֶׁבִּכְתָב וְשֶׁבְּעַל פֶּה כו' בְּרמ"ח מִצְוֹת עֲשֵׂה וְשס"ה לֹא תַעֲשֶׂה.

וְזֶהוּ כְּמוֹ טֶבַע הַשֶּׁמֶן שֶׁהוּא נִמְשָׁךְ וְיוֹרֵד וּמִתְעַלֵּם בְּכָל דָּבָר (כְּמוֹ שֶׁיִּתְבָּאֵר) עַל כֵּן נִמְשָׁךְ הַשֶּׁמֶן גַּם אַחַר הַפְּתִילָה לְחַבְּרוֹ בָּאוֹר.

וְהוּא עִנְיַן הַנַּ"ל בְּב' מַדְרֵיגוֹת דְּחָכְמָה אַחַת לַעֲשׂוֹת בְּחִינַת בִּיטּוּל הַיֵּשׁ לְאַיִן וְהוּא מַה שֶּׁיִּתְעוֹרֵר גַּם בַּגּוּף הִרְהוּר תְּשׁוּבָה בְּהַכְנָעָה עֲצוּמָה וְלֵב נִשְׁבָּר כו' וְעַל יְדֵי זֶה יָבֹא עִנְיַן כִּלְיוֹן הַפְּתִילָה בְּאֶשָּׁא אוּכָמָא שֶׁזֶּהוּ עִנְיַן הַצְּעָקָה וְהַעֲלָאָה בִּתְפִילָּה בִּשְׁפִיכַת נֶפֶשׁ לַהֲפוֹךְ הַמִּדּוֹת רָעוֹת שֶׁבַּלֵּב כו' כַּנַּ"ל וְזֶה נַעֲשֶׂה בְּסִיבַּת הַשֶּׁמֶן שֶׁנִּמְשָׁךְ בַּפְּתִילָה:

---

297. Psalms 147:5

298. See *Tanya* ch. 4, 8b.

299. In *Sefer HaKitzurim* by Rabbi Yosef Yizchak, which presents a paraphrase of each chapter of *Shaarei Orah*, the two kinds of abnegation deriving from *chochmah* are placed together in chapter Ten.

SUMMARY OF CHAPTER NINE

Returning to the image of the lamp, the *maamar* now discusses the relationship of the wick—the body and the animal soul—to the spiritual quality of the oil—*chochmah* and selflessness.

Why should oil, which is superior to the wick containing the two colors of the flame, be drawn after the wick, which would imply that the wick is superior?

To explain: The body is rooted in a realm that far transcends the root of the soul. The body's root stems from the radiance of *Tohu* which preceded *Tikkun* of the Divine Name [whose numerical value is] forty-five מ"ה. Thus, man is sustained by animals and vegetables [for their root transcends that of man]. When the body—the wick—is consumed, the sublime radiance of its source shines. This source precedes the source of spiritual oil, vested in Torah and mitzvot. Hence, the *dark radiance* causes the *bright radiance*. Nevertheless, the two colors are specifically produced by the oil, for without it the flame would dart away completely, or would totally consume the wick. In spiritual terms, the oil refers to the concealed radiance of Supernal *chochmah* (for the radiance is concealed within the oil—see chapters one, three and ten) which is revealed specifically through its manifestation in Torah and mitzvot

Accordingly, spiritual oil is the actual performance of Torah and mitzvot, which causes a *pure* flame to *gradually* consume the wick: in all, a well-structured lamp.

Now, although in chapter 3 it was established that spiritual oil would be *chochmah* and the selflessness it imparts by way of *hitbonenut* (contemplation)—primarily during prayer, as the *maamar* continued throughout chapters 4 and 5 – yet in chapter 6 this definition seems to shift to Torah and *mitzvot*, which prove to be spiritual oil by way of the explanation of chapters 7, 8. Chapter 9 appears to combine both explanations by saying that "oil refers to the concealment of the radiance of Supernal *chochmah* which is vested in Torah and *mitzvot*."

[This is apparently why in chapter 10 the discussion turns to *ratzo* and *shov* and their balanced combination necessary to serve G-d: One needs to combine both *ratzo*—the intense feelings in prayer, *teshuvah* and transforming one's negative qualities (*the dark radiance*), with *shov*—Torah and *mitzvot* (*the bright radiance*).

Thus, spiritual oil refers to both *hitbonenut* (prayer) and Torah/mitzvot: For to define *hitbonenut*, i.e. prayer, *teshuvah*, as spiritual oil would be the concept of *ratzo*, whereas to define Torah and mitzvot as the spiritual oil would be its counterpart, *shov*.]

INTRODUCTION TO CHAPTER TEN

The second level of selflessness relates to the bright radiance of the flame. It is an exalted level of total self-abnegation, yet it is expressed in Torah and *mitzvot.*

Hence one must combine both the intense feelings in prayer, the desire to exercise *teshuvah* and to change one's negative qualities (the lower dark flame)—with the upper bright flame which is manifest in *good deeds.*

The dark flame expresses "moving forward" *(ratzo)*, and the bright flame expresses "return" (*shov*). In one's service of G-d one needs a balanced combination of both. ...*Without intense feelings in prayer, moving forward, one cannot properly have the "return" of Torah and* mitzvot... *On the other hand... the ascent of the intense prayer without Torah study will not last at all.*

This balance and interdependence is illustrated by the nature of the lamp, in which oil and wick are interdependent, and the two kinds of flame likewise draw on each other.

10.
RATZO AND SHOV

CHOCHMAH LEVEL TWO

After the surge upwards of the natural soul, in a mode of *ratzo*,[300] "focusing one's heart on G-d,"[301] subsequently, "the spirit draws the spirit"[302]—which spontaneously causes a flow of radiance which descends below and vests specifically in a vessel.[303] This is termed *shov*, i.e., "these words which I command you" [*mitzvot*] which follows the love [of G-d] "with all your soul."

This is *sovev kol almin* expressed by Torah and *mitzvot*, manifested by the oil. For the consumption of the wick causes the primary flow of the light, and that the oil should be drawn and consumed. However, the oil that is drawn into the wick actually causes the clarity and brightness of the supernal radiance in the soul, [as it is derived] from *sovev kol almin*, the "bright radiance" described above.

This is the second aspect of *chochmah*, total *koach mah*, with the quality of the total Divine *Ayin*. This is the sense of lowness and humility, termed "absolute selflessness," that one's soul is utterly like dust to everything[304] because the person completely lacks any sense of their own self.

---

300. RATZO AND SHOV. In his vision of the Divine Chariot (the manifestation of Divine life force in the world of *Yetzirah*) the Prophet Ezekiel describes the actions of the animals pulling the chariot: They eagerly raise themselves up to catch a glimpse of the world of *Beriah* above the *rakia* (firmament) separating *Yetzirah* and *Beriah*. Then they hastily retreat in fear back to the world of *Yetzirah*. He renders this as "*vehachayot ratzo v'shov*"—"and the animals run and return" (*Ezekiel* 1:14).

Now the word *chayot* (lit. "wild animals") can also be read as *chiyut*—life force. The force enlivening all of the worlds is in a state of constant flux, of "running and returning." Life force is not static—it pulsates; indeed it is evidenced in the beating of the heart and the pulse, and in the inhalation and exhalation of the breath. (See *Sefer HaMaamarim 5696*, p. 25 ff.)

It would seem then that the ideal state is for the recipient of the life-force to rise up to a level where it completely transcends itself and loses its identity as it merges into the infinity of its source. After all, in doing so it reaches a far higher state of spirituality.

In fact this is not so, since "*not for chaos* [i.e., *ratzo* ending in the obliteration of self] *did He create* [*the world*], *rather He formed it to be settled* [to exist as a finite created world]," as stated in the text. However, since the soul and the light of the *sefirot* benefit from their association with the body and the vessel respectively, as explained above, this cannot be regarded as true selflessness (*bittul*). Genuine *bittul* is to fulfill what G-d wants irrespective

(י)

וְאָמְנָם אַחַר בְּחִינַת הַהַעֲלָאָה דְּנֶפֶשׁ הַטִּבְעִית בִּבְחִינַת רָצוֹא כְּמוֹ אִם יָשִׂים אֵלָיו לִבּוֹ כו׳ הֲרֵי רוּחַ אַיְיתֵי רוּחַ וְאַמְשִׁיךְ רוּחַ שֶׁמְּמֵילָא יָבֹא עַל יְדֵי זֶה בְּחִינַת הַמְשָׁכָה וִירִידַת הָאוֹר שֶׁבָּא בְּהִתְלַבְּשׁוּת לְמַטָּה בִּכְלִי דַּוְקָא שֶׁהוּא הַנִּקְרָא בְּחִינַת שׁוֹב שֶׁהוּא מַה שֶּׁכָּתוּב וְהָיוּ הַדְּבָרִים כו׳ אַחַר בְּכָל נַפְשְׁךָ כו׳.

וְהַיְינוּ בְּחִינַת סוֹבֵב כָּל עָלְמִין שֶׁבְּתוֹרָה וּמִצְוֹת כַּנַ״ל שֶׁנִּקְרָא שֶׁמֶן כִּי הֲרֵי כִּלְיוֹן הַפְּתִילָה גוֹרֵם עִיקַּר הַמְשָׁכַת הָאוֹר שֶׁיּוּמְשַׁךְ וְיִכְלֶה גַּם הַשֶּׁמֶן כַּנַ״ל וְאָמְנָם בְּמַה שֶּׁהַשֶּׁמֶן נִשְׁאָב בָּאוֹר הוּא הַגּוֹרֵם צְלִילַת וּבְהִירוּת הָאוֹר הָעֶלְיוֹן בַּנְּשָׁמָה מִבְּחִינַת סוֹבֵב כָּל עָלְמִין שֶׁנִּקְרָא נְהוֹרָא חִוְּורָא כַּנַ״ל.

וְהוּא מַדְרֵגָה הַב׳ דְּחָכְמָה כֹּחַ מָ״ה מַמָּשׁ כְּמוֹ שֶׁהִיא בִּבְחִינַת אַיִן מַמָּשׁ וְהוּא עִנְיַן הַשִּׁפְלוּת וְהָעֲנָוָה שֶׁנִּקְרָא בִּיטּוּל עַצְמִי שֶׁנַּפְשׁוֹ כֶּעָפָר לַכֹּל בְּעֶצֶם מִפְּנֵי הֶעְדֵּר הַרְגָּשַׁת עַצְמוֹ מִכֹּל וָכֹל כַּנַ״ל.

---

of any benefit that may accrue to the recipient. What G-d truly wants is "a dwelling place in the lower worlds" (*Midrash Tanchuma*, *Nasso*, ch. 16; *Tanya* ch. 36). Hence "its yearning should be in a way that will elicit a lofty light that will find expression in a manner of *shov*."

In the *maamar Acharei Mot 5649* Rabbi Shalom DovBer explains that yearning to transcend the physical is not only permissible but necessary. But the yearning must be premised on *shov*, "return," and imbued with *bittul*, selflessness.

Thus the Talmud (*Chagigah* 14b) relates that four sages "entered" the sublime sphere called *Pardes*, "Orchard," but only Rabbi Akiva emerged spiritually and emotionally intact. In the words of the Talmud, "Rabbi Akiva entered in peace and left in peace." By describing the manner in which he entered (which does not seem to be pertinent to the story), the Talmud implies that his peaceful emergence was the result of his peaceful entrance. I.e., since his initial motivation for entering the *Pardes* was predicated on *bittul* and the intention of *shov*, his *ratzo* ended in a positive way (*Likkutei Sichot* vol. 3, *Acharei Mot* p. 990).

301. See footnote 227.

302. See *Zohar* II:162b.

303. The "vessel" is Torah and *mitzvot*.

304. Liturgy, close of the Amidah.

Thus the two kinds of radiance are concealed in the oil itself, the dark radiance and the bright radiance. They emerge in the flames around the wick by the fact that the oil seeps into the wick and is drawn into the flame. For the clarity of the bright radiance depends specifically on the purity of the oil.

INTENSE PRAYER AND TESHUVAH VS. TORAH AND MITZVOT

Nonetheless, the main thing is the consumption of the wick, which elicits supernal radiance, due to the aforementioned reason—albeit that its brightness depends on the purity of the oil. In addition, it is the consumption of the wick that causes the oil to flow and to be consumed in the light. For the source of the wick—the natural soul—is higher than the level of *chochmah*.

Hence, without the "*ratzo*" of prayer, one cannot experience the "*shov*" of Torah and *mitzvot*. Similarly, one first needs *teshuvah*, and then good deeds.[305]

The proof for this is from the saying, "If one says 'I have only Torah study'—he does not even have Torah"[306]: Without the consumption of the wick, the oil will not flow to the flame at all. On the other hand, it is also true that the oil of Torah enables the flame to join with the wick, and without the oil the flame would not last even for a moment. In the same way, the ascent of *ratzo* in prayer without [the "*shov*" of] Torah study will not last at all.[307]

(Hence, the oil joins the flame to the wick, and the wick joins the oil to the flame. This is like man, who elevates the vegetable element, and subsequently the vegetable and animal elements elevate him.[308] The flame is made up of both qualities: the dark color, in which the wick and the oil are consumed, and the higher [bright] color that is drawn after the dark flame which consumes the wick and the oil. But its brightness is dependent on the purity of the oil (and on the extent to which the wick is consumed in the dark radiance.))

---

305. In accordance with the *Mishna* in *Avot* quoted above, that *teshuvah precedes* good deeds.

306. *Yevamot* 109b. In the Talmud this means one who claims only the virtue of Torah study at the expense of actually performing the *mitzvot*. In terms of this *maamar* it refers to Torah and *mitzvot—shov*, the "bright radiance," versus the "dark radiance" —the *ratzo* of prayer, *teshuvah* and self-transformation.

וְנִמְצָא דְשֶׁמֶן זֶה יֵשׁ בּוֹ מִב׳ הַגְּוָונִים דִנְהוֹרָא חִוְּורָא וְנְהוֹרָא אוּכָּמָא בְּהֶעְלֵם וְיָצְאוּ לְגִלוּי בְּאוֹר הַפְּתִילָה בְּמַה שֶׁנִּמְשָׁךְ בַּפְּתִילָה וְנִשְׁאָב בָּאוֹר שֶׁהֲרֵי בְּהִירוּת אוֹר הָעֶלְיוֹן תָּלוּי בִּצְלִילַת הַשֶּׁמֶן דַּוְקָא כַּנַּ״ל.

וְעִם כָּל זֶה הֲרֵי הָעִיקָר הוּא כִּלְיוֹן הַפְּתִילָה שֶׁהוּא הַגּוֹרֵם הַמְשָׁכַת הָאוֹר הָעֶלְיוֹן מִטַּעַם הַנַּ״ל רַק שֶׁבְּהִירָתוֹ תָּלוּי בִּצְלִילַת הַשֶּׁמֶן לְבָד וְגַם הוּא הַסִּיבָּה לְהַמְשָׁכַת הַשֶּׁמֶן וְכַלּוֹתוֹ בָּאוֹר כַּנַּ״ל הַטַּעַם שֶׁשֹּׁרֶשׁ הַפְּתִילָה שֶׁהוּא הַנֶּפֶשׁ הַטִּבְעִית לְמַעְלָה מִבְּחִינַת חָכְמָה.

וְעַל כֵּן בְּלֹא בְּחִינַת רָצוֹא דִתְפִילָּה אִי אֶפְשָׁר לִהְיוֹת בְּחִינַת שׁוֹב דְתוֹרָה וּמִצְוֹת כַּנַּ״ל וְכֵן תְּשׁוּבָה וְאַחַר כַּךְ מַעֲשִׂים טוֹבִים.

וּרְאָיָה לָזֶה מִמַּה שֶׁאָמְרוּ הָאוֹמֵר אֵין לִי אֶלָּא תוֹרָה אֲפִילוּ תוֹרָה אֵין לוֹ כְּמוֹ שֶׁבְּלֹא כִּלְיוֹן הַפְּתִילָה אֵין הַשֶּׁמֶן נִמְשָׁךְ בָּאוֹר כְּלָל אֲבָל גַּם זֶה אֱמֶת דְּעַל יְדֵי הַשֶּׁמֶן דְתוֹרָה הוּא הַסִּיבָּה לְחִיבּוּר הָאוֹר בַּפְּתִילָה וּבִלְעָדוֹ אֵין קִיוּם לָאוֹר בַּפְּתִילָה כְּלָל אֲפִילוּ רֶגַע כַּנַּ״ל וְכַךְ הוּא הַעֲלָאָה דְרָצוֹא בִּתְפִילָּה בְּלֹא תוֹרָה שֶׁאֵינוֹ מִתְקַיֵּים כְּלָל כַּיָּדוּעַ וְדַי לַמֵּבִין:

(וְנִמְצָא שֶׁהַשֶּׁמֶן מְחַבֵּר הָאוֹר בַּפְּתִילָה וְהַפְּתִילָה מְחַבֵּר הַשֶּׁמֶן בָּאוֹר וְזֶה כְּמוֹ אָדָם שֶׁמַּעֲלֶה אֶת הַצּוֹמֵחַ וְאַחַר כַּךְ הַצּוֹמֵחַ וְחַי מַעֲלֵהוּ מִטַּעַם הַנַּ״ל וְהָאוֹר מוּרְכָּב מִשְּׁנֵיהֶם בֵּין בְּגַוָּון הַשָּׁחוֹר שֶׁכָּלֶה בּוֹ הַפְּתִילָה וְהַשֶּׁמֶן בֵּין בְּגַוָּון הָעֶלְיוֹן שֶׁנִּמְשָׁךְ אַחַר הַשָּׁחוֹר הַמְכַלֶּה לַפְּתִילָה וְשֶׁמֶן רַק שֶׁבְּהִירָתוֹ הוּא לְפִי זַכּוּת הַשֶּׁמֶן וּצְלִילָתוֹ (וְגַם לְפִי עֶרֶךְ כִּלְיוֹן הַפְּתִילָה בַּגַּוָּון הַשָּׁחוֹר כו׳):)

---

307. Thus, genuine divine service consists of both "wick and oil," in accordance to the manner that their functions are explained above, in such great detail, for both are the most vital components of a lamp. And in human terms, the wick corresponds to prayer and *teshuvah—ratzo*, while the oil corresponds to actual performance of Tirah and *mitzvot—shov.*

308. By subsequently utilizing the energy gained from their sustenance for Torah and *mitzvot.* See footnotes 261 and 280.

SUMMARY
OF CHAPTER TEN

The oil, which is *chochmah*, contains the two colors of radiance. These are: 1) the abnegation of the self before the Divine *Ayin*—the consumption of the wick (*dark radiance*); 2) the elevation of the Animal Soul—through lowliness and humility, termed "essential *bittul*"—which elicits G-dliness to be vested into the vessel—a pure light (*bright radiance*). These two levels are revealed both in the consumption of the wick and in the clarity of the radiance. Hence, the oil causes the flame to cleave to the wick (benefit one, above ch. 1); and the oil drawn to the wick produces clear radiance (benefit two).

In one's service of G-d one needs a balanced combination of *ratzo* and *shov*. The radiance of Torah (*bright radiance, shov*) is preceded by prayer (*dark radiance, ratzo*). One needs to combine both *ratzo*—the intense feelings in prayer, *teshuvah* and transforming one's negative qualities (*the dark radiance*), with *shov*—Torah and *mitzvot* (*the bright radiance*).

For if not for the consumption of the wick (*the dark radiance*), the oil (*the bright radiance*) would not be drawn.

This balance and interdependence is illustrated by the nature of the lamp, in which oil and wick are interdependent, and the two kinds of flame likewise draw on each other.

Thus ends the first ten chapters of the *maamar* with a depiction of the subtle balance necessary in the service of G-d.

BRIEF BIOGRAPHY

BRIEF BIOGRAPHY OF RABBI DOVBER SCHNEURI, THE MITTELER REBBE

Adapted from the writings of Rabbi Yosef Yitzchak of Lubavitch

Rabbi DovBer, the second of the seven Chabad Rebbes, was the eldest son of Rabbi Schneur Zalman of Liadi, founder of Chabad.

Rabbi Schneur Zalman, known as the Alter Rebbe, provided the seminal points of Chabad philosophy. Rabbi DovBer, known as the Mitteler Rebbe,[1] built upon his father's structure, expounding, developing and articulating his father's words. He could spend thirty pages explaining one page of his father's.[2]

A child prodigy, by age sixteen he was an expert on Talmud and Jewish law; he was fluent in the secrets of Kabbala and Chasidut.

His was an extraordinarily vigorous mind, such that while delivering his discourses to his perfectly silent audiences, he

1. "The Middle Rebbe." He received this designation after his passing, during the leadership years of his son-in-law, the Tzemach Tzedek. At that time, the Tzemach Tzedek was known as "the Rebbe"; Rabbi Schneur Zalman was known as "the Old Rebbe" (Alter Rebbe); and Rabbi Dovber was known as "the Middle Rebbe" (Mitteler Rebbe).

2. The Alter Rebbe is known as the *Chochmah* of Chabad, while the Mitteler Rebbe is known as the *binah* of Chabad. His style of teaching is also known as *rechovot hanahar*, "the expanses of the river."

(*Chochmah* and *binah* are terms used in Kabbala and Chasidut to refer to the two stages within the intellectual process. *chochmah* (insight) is the initial flash of insight, the "aha" moment, which is like an undeveloped seed that unfolds in *Binah* (comprehension), where the seminal point of *chochmah* is built up and fleshed out.)

The Rebbe's grandson, Rabbi Shmuel (fourth Chabad Rebbe), related that his grandfather had a *kapelya*, a musical group of musicians and singers.

"Grandfather," said Rabbi Shmuel, "needed to conduct himself with great expansiveness and with all things that create the opening of the mind and heart, since Grandfather is the power of *Binah* within Chabad Chasidut."

would often say "*Sha! Sha!,*" silencing some disturbance of which only he was aware. His great-grandson Rabbi Shalom DovBer (fifth Chabad Rebbe) explained that he was quieting the overwhelming flood of thoughts streaming from his mind.

"When my father-in-law contemplated Chasidic teachings," the Tzemach Tzedek reported, "his soul was in a different world. His body would then receive sustenance directly from his thoughts of the Divine."[3]

His grandson Rabbi Shmuel (fourth Chabad Rebbe) related that his grandfather "wrote with extraordinary speed. When he reached the fortieth or fiftieth line on the page, the ink at the top of the page was still wet.[4] When Grandfather wrote Chasidic discourses his hand was directly connected to his power of thought and so he wrote at the speed of his thoughts."

DEVOTION

The rivers of elucidation that he unleashed demonstrate more than his brilliance; they reveal the seriousness with which he undertook his role as teacher—and the love he had for his flock.

He saw it as his life's mission to bring Chasidic teachings to the people. It was his wish that when two chasidim would meet they would speak about the supernal attributes of *Arich* and *Atik*.[5] He expected of his students that they understand the Divine level of *Ketter* as well as they are familiar with their five fingers.

He was wont to say: "I take upon myself to solve all the questions. Wherever I shall be,[6] I will help chasidim understand those things they find difficult."

---

3. The Tzemach Tzedek also said of him that had he lived in the times of the Geonim (589-1038 C.E.) he would have been like one of them. His chasid Rabbi Eliyah Yosef of Dribin related that his Rebbe's mastery of Talmud was even greater than his mastery of Chasidut.)

4. "Chasidim thought that this was done by "*hashba'at hakulmus* [adjuring the pen —causing it to write on its own in some mystical way]." G-d forbid— Grandfather would not make use of such a thing."

5. Two of the most exalted Kabbalistic levels explained in Chasidic teachings. See Schochet's *Mystical Concepts in Chassidus* (Kehot).

6. Referring to the different levels of ascent in *Gan Eden.*

He was an incredible teacher. He was said to have the power to penetrate the soul of even "a block of wood."[7]

During the duration of one Shabbos he was capable of delivering Chasidic discourses many times, each discourse lasting for a few hours.

He wrote and published a number of volumes that clarified in great detail the path of Chasidic worship. This is especially true of his book Tract on Ecstasy and Gate of Return and Prayer, in which he reveals the inner workings of every person, both the positive and the negative. It was said that he writes from the perspective of one "sitting inside the chambers of our hearts."

He even wrote a number of "customized" books, directed to specific individuals, to help them in their Divine service and their understanding of Chasidut.

So invested was he in the spiritual condition of his students that their actions literally affected his health. When a young man once asked him for a path of correction for his misdeeds, the Rebbe rolled up his sleeve and showed the man his arm: "My flesh cleaves to the bone—dry like a tree. All of this is from your misdeeds." Such was the love and devotion of the Rebbe to his students.

He not only preached to his chasidim, he provided a living example. He was a master of prayer. He prayed with joy, with an inner silence and delight.

He was a man of miracles. It was said of the Rebbe's family that for them miracles were the norm. The Rebbe did not consider miracles to be anything wondrous and he performed them off the cuff. He would say that such and such would occur and so it would be.[8]

---

7. Paradoxically, he was barely able to relate to his students. He was on a completely different spiritual plane. He had only a vague notion of what his students were about and yet was able to train them effectively.

8. Lag b'Omer was one of the Rebbe's special festivals. The chasidim would go out into the field with the Rebbe. The Rebbe would not have a meal then but he would drink spirits, although his doctors had prohibited him from doing so. At that time, the chasidim saw many miracles—primarily in regard to the birth of children. Chasidim would wait all year for Lag b'Omer.

And he was a man of deep humility. When his son-in-law, the Tzemach Tzedek, was asked for a term to describe his father-in-law, he used one word: "Humble." From the time his father passed away, he would be called up to the Torah only once a year—together with the children on Simchat Torah. He was embarrassed in the presence of the Torah scroll....

SINCERITY

He sought and demanded sincerity. Compromise was a complete stranger to him. He is quoted as saying: "Anyone can speak; but to speak the truth—the eyes must pop out of their sockets...."

The depth of his sincerity, humility and devotion is demonstrated in the following story, related by Rabbi Yosef Yitzchak (a descendant of the Mitteler Rebbe and sixth Chabad Rebbe):

One summer, during one of his travels, the Rebbe lodged at a hotel not far from the city of Smargon. The weather was pleasant, and the Rebbe decided to stay for a week.

News of the Rebbe's decision spread and a large group of people converged upon the hotel to see him for "*yechidut*," a private one-on-one talk.

One day, as hundreds of people were standing waiting their turn for *yechidut*, the Rebbe suddenly instructed his attendants to close the door. He said he would be unable to receive any more guests.

The chasidim standing in the courtyard waiting their turn, as well as the chasidim who were studying the Rebbe's latest discourse,[9] assumed that the Rebbe was exhausted by all his visitors and that he had taken a break to rest up and refresh.

Half an hour later, the attendant Reb Zalman emerged with eyes red from crying. He seemed extremely distressed. He approached the prominent chasidim and whispered some-

9. That was the protocol during each of the Rebbe's travels: first the chasid would study and review the discourse the Rebbe had most recently said and only then would he enter *yechidut*.

thing in their ears. His words alarmed the chasidim and their faces began to change colors. A sense of foreboding overcame the chasidim.

One or two hours later, a few prominent chasidim entered the hotel and were able to hear the Rebbe reciting chapters of Psalms, pouring out his heart and crying profusely from the depths of his holy heart. A few of them fainted out of sheer anguish not knowing what had caused this great fear to fall upon their Rebbe—why in middle of the day, a weekday, he would stop receiving guests and suddenly engage in such an intense session of contrition and tears.

When the crowd standing in the courtyard heard the tumult they began reciting Psalms themselves and crying from the depths of their hearts.

The Rebbe, after concluding his recitation of Psalms, began preparing himself for the afternoon prayer but was so exhausted by reading Psalms that he was forced to lie on his bed for over an hour to recuperate.

He then recited the afternoon prayer in the manner that it is recited during the days between Rosh Hashanah and Yom Kippur.

After the afternoon prayer, the Rebbe went out to the courtyard and delivered a discourse. He said that tears cleanse the person of the negative words that may have passed his lips and the negative thoughts that may have crossed his mind. He explained the great benefit of reciting words of Torah and Psalms.

This discourse shook the chasidim to their core and roused something deep within them. Even many years later, the event remained firmly implanted in their minds.

The next day, the Rebbe was extremely weak and was forced to lie on his bed. Only on the following day did he once again begin to receive visitors.

A few days later, one of the esteemed chasidim, Rabbi Pinchas of Shklov, asked the Rebbe about the incident.

The Rebbe became distressed for a moment, then said:

"When people come to me for *yechidut* and reveal the afflictions of the depths of their hearts, every person according to his situation—I have to find that flaw as it exists within myself, even on the most refined level. I cannot answer a person and recommend a true path of correction before I have rectified this flaw within myself. Only then can I provide some advice and a protocol for rehabilitation.

"On that day, a man came to me, and confided something that was so shocking, that I was unable to find within myself—*chas v'shalom,*[10] *chas v'shalom*—even a hint of a hint of such a thing, even on the most refined level. It occurred to me that perhaps *chas v'shalom* and *chas v'shalom* this was a reflection of some hidden negativity within me that was buried deep, deep within. This thought shook the very essence of my soul and caused me to return to G-d from the depths of my heart."

* * *

BIRTH

Rabbi Schneur Zalman of Liadi, founder of Chabad philosophy, was married to his wife, Rebbetzin Rivkah, in the year 1760.

Thirteen years later, during a visit with his master, he asked that he be blessed with the birth of a male child. Until then he had been blessed only with daughters.

His master, Rabbi DovBer, the Maggid of Mezrich, successor to the Baal Shem Tov, turned to him and said: "How does one merit a lad? Through guests."[11] By fulfilling the precept of taking in guests, Rabbi Schneur Zalman would merit the birth of a male child.

The Maggid proceeded to relate that the birth of the Baal Shem Tov, whose parents were barren, occurred also in the merit of extraordinary hospitality.[12]

---

10. "Heaven forefend."

11. A midrash-like play on the verse (Psalms 119:9) "*Ba'meh yi'zakeh na'ar et orcho (lishmor kidvarecha),*" which in its literal sense means, "How does a lad make his path meritorious? (By fulfilling Your Word)." *Orcho,* "his path," can also mean "his guest."

12. The Baal Shem Tov's parents, Rabbi Eliezer and Sarah, lived in a small village where they made a nice living. They used only a small portion of their income for themselves—the rest was spent on hospitality. Every Shabbat, twenty to thirty guests graced their table. One Shabbos, a guest showed up in town and made his way to the home of Rabbi Eliezer. Rabbi

In 1773, two days before his passing, the Maggid spoke to Rabbi Schneur Zalman from his bed: "During the last three days before a person returns his soul, he can see the Divine word that exists within each physical object." That night, he taught Rabbi Schneur Zalman the protocol of study for the night preceding a circumcision. He also described the protocol for the day of the circumcision itself as well the procedure for the Friday night that precedes it (known as *Shalom Zachar*). He said to him:

"He who serves G-d can see[13]: A son will be born to you, and you shall call him by my name. On the night before his circumcision, remember and mention the teachings that I have taught you tonight."

The next day, on the 19th of Kislev, Rabbi DovBer's soul returned to its Maker.

A year later, on the ninth of Kislev, a son was born to Rabbi Schneur Zalman.[14]

He was named DovBer.

EARLY YEARS

From a very young age, DovBer was recognized as a genius. He was extremely studious. In school, instead of reviewing his studies, he would listen in as the teacher taught the older students. He absorbed new concepts like a sponge and retained them in his phenomenal memory. Returning home from school, he would review what he had overheard being taught

---

Eliezer served him as he did all others. The other guests, however, taunted Rabbi Eliezer for serving a man who obviously desecrated the Shabbos. (The closest town was further than what one is allowed to walk on Shabbos.) A conflicted Rabbi Eliezer went off to a private room and cried. But he quickly realized that his absence would make the new guest uncomfortable, so he went out and honored the man even more than he had before. On Sunday afternoon, when the guests would customarily depart, the mysterious guest told Rabbi Eliezer that he was in fact Elijah the Prophet and that he had been sent from heaven to test Rabbi Eliezer. Rabbi Eliezer had passed the test and would therefore merit a son. So was born the Baal Shem Tov (*Sefer Hasichot 5697* p. 161).

13. A play on the words "*chazon Ovadiah*," "vision of Obadiah." (Obadiah, the name of a prophet, can also be read as two words that mean "he who serves G-d.")

14. Rabbi Schneur Zalman provided a special linen cloth with which to wrap the child for the first time after being washed.

to the older class and so became fluent in many chapters of the Torah and the Prophets. Despite his devotion to study, he was a happy and lively child.

He was a swift and talented writer. In beautiful script, he would transcribe his father's teachings, stories and conduct, as well as the stories he heard from his mother and the elder chasidim who had been students of the Baal Shem Tov and the Maggid. He wrote of his father's travels; his father's first and second arrest; the move from Liozna to Liadi; fleeing from Napoleon[15]; and other episodes.

At the age of seven he would ask his father questions like "Why are some rich people so arrogant?" (His father replied that the spiritual "chamber" of wealth is situated between *Gan Eden* and *Gehenom*. This chamber has two doors, one leading to *Gan Eden* and one leading to *Gehenom*. Wealth can be heaven for one, hell for another. If it used for *tzedakah*, Torah and *mitzvot* then it is *Gan Eden*. If it is used for worldly things or horded—the wealth itself becomes a hell.")

Such were the conversations that took place between father and son.

EYES THAT CANNOT SEE

[As a child, he displayed a flair for homiletic interpretation, much like his namesake.]

Returning from school one day, he noticed a group of chasidim who were waiting to be received by his father. Among them was the jovial chasid Rabbi Shmuel Munkes, to whom DovBer was especially drawn. As he approached, he heard Rabbi Shmuel addressing Rabbi Yosef Kol-Bo, a wealthy chasid from Shklov: "Why are you depressed?"

"The financial situation is not good," replied the businessman.

Hearing this, the child turned to Rabbi Shmuel and asked: "Why do you ask such a question? There is a verse that clearly provides the answer: *'Their depression*[16] *stems from silver*

---

15. See *Rabbi Schneur Zalman of Liadi* (Kehot, ed. 2002), p. 225 ff.

16. A play on the verse (Psalms 115:4) *atzabeihem kessef v'zahav,* "their idols are of

and gold, the handiwork of mortals'—because they are blind and foolish and think that silver and gold is gained through the work of man and his efforts.

"They think that the more they work—running to Leipzig and to Koeningsburg—the more will they increase their silver and gold.

"They fool themselves and come to a point where *'they have a mouth but cannot speak'*—they speak words of Chasidut but these words have no effect on them, they are without meaning. *'They have eyes, but do not see'* Divine providence; *'they have ears'* but perceive only the external and so cannot *'smell'*—they cannot sense the inner working of things."

His teacher, Rabbi Avraham of Lyepli (who, thanks to a blessing he received from the Alter Rebbe, lived over one hundred years), related the following:

"I once taught him the Talmudic passage that says that Rabbah was most meticulous with the *mitzvah* of *tzitzit* [more than any other *mitzvah*]. The child smiled and said:

"'How could it be that Rabbah was not absolutely meticulous with the mitzvah of *tefillin* or other *mitzvot*? There is no doubt that he fulfilled every *mitzvah* with utmost meticulousness and precision.'

"I then asked him what indeed the passage meant—and he said: '*Tzizit* was the mitzvah through which the light of his soul was best expressed.[17]'"

On another occasion, when he was ten years old, he was present at a *farbrengen* (an informal Chasidic get-together), which he would attend almost without exception. The chasidim had offered a homiletic interpretation of a *Mishnah*

---

silver and gold, the handiwork of mortals. They have mouths but cannot speak; they have ears but cannot hear; they have noses but cannot smell...." *Atazbeihem* (idols) contains the root *etzev*, depression.

17. "The *mitzvot* are 'broad vessels' through which the light of the soul can shine. Each mitzvah is a specific type of gate through which the soul is revealed. For Rabbah, the mitzvah of *tzitzit* was the special gate through which his soul was most revealed. This mitzvah gave life to all the *mitzvot* he fulfilled." (The Talmud (*Shabbos* 118b) uses the word *zahir*, which in its literal sense means meticulous. However, the Rebbe interpreted it to mean "shine.")

(*Kidushin* 28b) and later asked him if he approved of what was said. He replied: "You did not interpret the second half of the *Mishnah*, which states that *A pledge to on High is like "giving over" [a legal transaction] to an ordinary person*:

"If only our pledge to on High—our desire to ascend spiritually—would be as earnest as our devotion—our 'givenoverness' to ordinary matters."[18]

HEARING THINGS

His spiritual sensitivity, even at the young age of twelve, was extraordinary.

Along with the rest of the congregation, he would listen to the weekly Torah reading read by his father. One year, the Alter Rebbe was out of town for the Shabbat when the Torah portion *Ki Tavo* was read (about two weeks before Rosh Hashanah). *Ki Tavo* includes a section of admonition, in which the Jewish people are told of the horrific consequences of veering from the Torah's laws. After hearing the admonition read by the substitute Torah reader, the child was so emotionally upset that it was suspected he would be unable to fast on Yom Kippur.[19]

Later, the chasidim asked him, "Why were you not disturbed when the admonition was read in past years?"

The Rebbe explained that in previous years his father read the Torah, and "when Father reads, no curses are heard."

BAR MITZVAH

In the year 1787, the Rebbe reached the age of Bar-Mitzvah. His father was quite excited about this event. For three weeks prior, he delivered Chasidic discourses twice on each Shabbat.

---

18. Another *Mishnah* in the eyes of the young Dovber (Shabbos 19:6): *He who circumcises but does not peel off [the membrane] is considered as if he had not circumcised.* Dovber explained this as follows: One who wishes to fulfill the mitzvah of circumcision in the spiritual sense—circumcising the foreskin of the heart—and begins to serve G-d and to awaken his love and fear of Him, but who has not "peeled back"—he does not work hard on the service of turn from bad and do good, he imagines that he is already circumcised and can now walk in the paths of Divine service—it is as if he did not circumcise.

19. Although he was only twelve, he would have had to fast since it is customary to fast on the three fast days that precede Bar-mitzvah.

On Thursday, the Ninth of Kislev, many candles were lit in the shul to create a festive mood. The Alter Rebbe himself read from the Torah Thursday morning and took the third *aliyah* for himself.

After the prayers, the Alter Rebbe delivered a short teaching about the nature of Torah and then turned to his son and instructed him to deliver the Torah thought that he had instructed him to prepare. The Mitteler Rebbe spoke for a few moments about the different types of relationships with G-d —that of the simple person and that of the intellectual.

After his son's talk, the Alter Rebbe was elated. His son's words had placed him into a deep state of *dveykut* ("attachment," "ecstasy"). The crowd was completely silent; all eyes were on the Alter Rebbe. After a while, the Alter Rebbe began to sing his famous melody, "The Four Stanzas," which correspond to the four letters in G-d's Name (y-h-v-h) and the four "worlds" (*Atzilut*, *Beriah*, *Yetzirah*, and *Asiyah*). He sang each stanza twice; the fourth, he sang many times.

When the Alter Rebbe finished singing, he ate some honey bread and drank a cup of spirits. Food and drink was then served to the joyous guests.

After the evening prayers, a meal was served and the Alter Rebbe delivered a Chasidic discourse. The chasidim "*farbrenged*" all night. This was the first Bar-Mitzvah in the Alter Rebbe's family.

That Friday night, the Alter Rebbe studied the Book of *Zohar* with his son. He said that he had heard in the name of the Baal Shem Tov that the Torah reading during the afternoon prayers on Shabbos is most sublime.

Indeed the Mitteler Rebbe was called to the Torah for the first time during the afternoon Torah reading on Shabbos.[20]

---

20. The chasidim, who had not been present during the father-son Friday night conversation, were at a loss to explain why the Mitteler Rebbe was not called up to the Torah during the morning reading. That he had not been called up on Thursday they were able to explain based on various halachic considerations. But why skip the morning Reading? This they did not know.

They approached the Mitteler Rebbe's younger brother, Chaim Avraham, who was then six or seven years old, and asked him if he knew the answer to this

MASHPIA

He was a devoted student of his father's teachings and yearned constantly to hear new insights. However, since he had a weak heart and weak lungs from a young age, the Alter Rebbe would deliver Chasidic discourses to his son privately to improve the young man's poor health. These private sessions would revive the weak DovBer.

In 1788 he married Rebbetzin Sheina, the daughter of a poor *melamed.* The fellow had five daughters whom he had trouble marrying off due to his poverty. The Alter Rebbe offered his son to the *melamed* as a son-in-law so that the *melamed's* other daughters would become desirable to the masses....

When he was all but sixteen years old, the Alter Rebbe placed an enormous responsibility upon his shoulders. He gave him the task of overseeing the development and education of the "sitters," the young married chasidim, who lived in Liozna and spent all their time in study, prayer, and spiritual development. He was also to maintain a correspondence with those who lived in other cities and spent their days in study supported by their fathers or fathers-in-law.

He took to his new responsibility with complete devotion. Once, during a *farbrengen* with his students, he spoke passionately about the importance of the service of the heart and contemplative prayer. Speaking from his heart, he poured out his soul.

His excited talk left him ill for a number of days. One of the elder chasidim, who was present at the *farbrengen,* asked the Rebbe why he has spoken so passionately knowing the ill effect it would have on his health.

The Rebbe answered: "When I thought about the mandate that was given to my soul when it descended to my body, as it affects me and all future generations, as well as the enormous responsibility that was placed upon me in regard to a

riddle. Chaim Avraham then explained to them what he had overheard that Friday night; and the chasidim were puzzled no more.

student and his descendants—how could I have contained the feelings of my heart?!"

At first he focused on teaching the philosophy of Chasidut and later began training his students in the art of character refinement and love for one's fellow.

His father once said: "Love for one's fellow is the vessel for love for G-d." Commenting on the impact of this statement, the Mitteler Rebbe said: "This statement implanted love for one's fellow even in the small fingernail of the small finger."

He once told his students: "Whoever does not engage in matters of Divine worship with an inner feeling and fools himself about his spiritual condition is fooling only himself. And how foolish it is to fool a fool...."

This pointed remark, said Rabbi Yosef Yitzchak, "opened a window in the consciousness of his students through which the sunlight of Divine worship in the Chasidic fashion that the Alter Rebbe had revealed shone through. It was now obvious to them that a real chasid was one who studies Chasidic concepts as they relate to transforming one's nature—and that only after becoming a pure vessel, rinsed with the tears of prayer, can one become a receptacle for the philosophy of Chasidut."

LUBAVITCH

After his father's passing in 1812, the Mitteler Rebbe lived temporarily in the city of Kremenchug. Later, he chose to make his dwelling in the city of Lubavitch, the city that was to house the Chabad movement for the next one hundred years. For three months he traveled from Kremenchug to Lubavitch, stopping in each city along the way. In each place he would teach Chasidic discourses and receive individual chasidim for *yechidut*. He was received with great honor wherever he went. Government officials had been instructed by the offices of the Ministry of Interior in Petersburg to accord Rabbi DovBer the utmost respect in gratitude for all the good his father had done for the country in its battle against Napoleon.

The itinerary for the trip was planned ahead of time. The

governors of Poltova, Minsk and Mogilev were instructed to provide first-rate carriages and hospitality for Rabbi DovBer, his family and entourage.

When he arrived in Lubavitch, he made his way to an empty plot of land, whose houses had burnt down two years prior, and declared:

"Fifty eight years ago, when my father was ten years old and studied with the *tzaddik* and *chasid* Rabbi Yisachar Dov—they studied in a shul that stood on this plot of land.

"While I prepared myself for this trip, my father told me that when I arrive in Lubavitch I should establish my residence on this spot."

His arrival in Lubavitch, on the 18th of Elul in the year 1813, along with part of his family and thousands of chasidim, made a huge impact all over White Russia and Lithuania. Everyone knew of the Alter Rebbe's contribution to the war against the French and so the government officials as well as the landowners looked kindly upon the chasidim.

Masses of people streamed to Lubavitch from every city and village.

Count Tchekovsky, who owned Lubavitch and the surrounding villages, instructed the manager of his estate to provide wood from his forests to build houses for the Rebbe and his family.

Throughout the winter months, the Mitteler Rebbe's fame spread all over the cities of Lithuania and White Russia and the number of visitors to Lubavitch kept growing. It was a time of great joy and pride for the chasidim of White Russia and Lithuania.

WITH THE OPPONENTS

When the Russo-Franco war quieted down in the winter of 1813, the opponents of Chasidut began sending spies to the Chasidic cities in order to campaign against Chasidut and to discourage the Jewish populace from becoming students of the Mitteler Rebbe. Although they were unsuccessful, they did not despair, especially since they knew of the Mitteler Rebbe's humble and soft-spoken ways.

But as soon as the Mitteler Rebbe settled in Lubavitch, he instructed his chasidim to refrain from interacting in any way with the opponents. He told them to build their own synagogues and not to enter those of the opponents even on rare occasions. There were times that the Rebbe instructed those chasidim living in cities that did not have a quorum of ten chasidim, to pray alone and to listen to the reading of the Torah from behind the door or window of the synagogue.

The chasidim were not to enter into any debates with the opponents. When the Rebbe heard of any clash between the two groups he would censor the chasidim involved and forbid them from coming to Lubavitch.

The Rebbe himself followed his own rules. When he met with opponents regarding communal matters, he would restrict the conversation to bettering the economic condition of the Jewish populace. No man dared to raise the issue of Chasidut and its practices.

This strategy of disengagement worked. The opponents eventually despaired of impeding the growth of Chasidut.

During the war years, Torah study had been in decline and the general mood was down. But with the Rebbe's arrival in Lubavitch, his guidance and vision, a revival of Chasidic life began to take place.

During his leadership, the amount of chasidim tripled. This was partly due to the fact that some of the chasidim were exceptional orators and to the fact that the Mitteler Rebbe's teachings contained extensive explanation and were thus understandable to most listeners.

In the first year of the new Rebbe's leadership, he gained fifteen thousand new chasidim. In the next year, the entire Chernigov region had become Chabad chasidim.

CHASIDIM

The Mitteler Rebbe's chasidim were known for their spiritual maturity. When their Rebbe would speak about character change, they would feel actual shame. When the Rebbe once spoke about one who is good on the outside but bad on the inside, tens of his chasidim fainted on the spot.

His devoted chasidim were people whose entire life was Torah and Divine worship; all worldly concerns were to them an afterthought.

The relationship between the Rebbe and his chasidim was legend. The renowned Professor Heibenthal once passed through Lubavitch on his way to a leading astronomer who lived in a villa near Lubavitch. Heibenthal entered the hall in which the Rebbe was saying a Chasidic discourse. When he saw how absorbed and attached the chasidim were as they listened to their Rebbe—each one frozen in place, some mouths agape, others wide-eyed, in utter silence—he commented that such concentration and absorption is possible only with the power of the soul.

COMMUNAL WORK

Not only did the Mitteler Rebbe carry on and expound upon the torch of Chabad philosophy handed to him by his father, he also continued in his father's path of communal work.

Throughout his leadership years, he concentrated on bettering the condition of his brethren, who were then at the mercy of an anti-Semitic, Czarist regime. Their rights were limited; their incomes meager.

Like his father, the Rebbe encouraged his brethren to leave behind the unstable business ventures they had until then embraced, and to settle in villages to work the land and to learn other manual labors. This way their livelihood would be gained calmly and would not distract them from Divine worship.

The following is an excerpt of a letter he wrote regarding working the land:

> *...Jobs are scant; poverty is rampant. People are wandering afar—so it is obvious what becomes of them.... ...he who has money loses it and falls downward....*
>
> *...Let them purchase good land from the landowners according to the government; and whether it is small or large, G-d will certainly grant a blessing upon the land, and there will at least be enough to feed the family. Certainly they will*

> *hire non-Jewish workers to work the land for the first two or three years until they will become accustomed to this work themselves. Let not this work be despised, G-d forbid, for on our land in the Land of Israel, all of our occupation was in the field and vineyard...why are we different from our forefathers...?*
>
> *...When I visited the steppes, I saw with my own eyes the work of the Jews with their wives and children, working in the fields with vigor and enthusiasm—the labor is sweet to them all week long. The boys until age thirteen study in the cheder, while those who are not successful [in study] work in the field. These people are sated with bread and satisfied with their lot—there is no sadness among them.*
>
> *...True they will never be rich or be able to live lavishly with expensive clothing and jewelry, but their basic needs are assured....*

He also devoted himself to supporting the settlement of the Land of Israel. In 1823, he was the first to found a settlement in the holy city of Hebron. He supported its settlers with handsome donations and bought one or two rooms adjacent to the Avraham Avinu Synagogue from its *Sefardic* owners, to be used by his followers as an *Ashkenazic* (Chasidic) synagogue.[21]

There were certain chasidim who he encouraged to remain in Russia and those that he encouraged to migrate to the Land of Israel. Among the latter group was Reb Yisrael Yaffe, the printer from Kopust.[22] However, Reb Yisrael did not want to leave his Rebbe—he wanted to remain with him and continue to hear his teachings. The Rebbe therefore promised to send him transcripts of his discourses—and so it was. (The Rebbe's great-grandson, Rabbi Shalom DovBer, later (circa 1890) purchased these writings from the descendants of Reb Yisrael.)

---

21. The Rebbe's synagogue also bore the name *Avraham Avinu Synagogue,* thus creating two synagogues by the same name. It remains unclear exactly how large his synagogue was, or how many rooms it consisted of.

22. It was for this Reb Yisrael that the Rebbe wrote the book *Pirush Hamilot,* Chasidic explanations of the prayers.

NEW RULES

The woes of his people, both spiritual and physical, were too much for his frail health. He grew weak and was no longer able to receive his chasidim for private audience. He instructed them to direct all of their questions to his brother, Rabbi Chaim Avraham, and to his son-in-law, the Tzemach Tzedek:

"...All of you know of my extremely weak health and, primarily, that I do not have the strength to bear any pain or grief of any person...

Each person comes here with deeply troubling issues—whether it is a negative trait [he wishes to correct], or matters relating to children, livelihood, or a need for protection from adversaries, or a need for a letter against those who are encroaching upon his livelihood and other matters of disputes between man and his fellow. And primarily, they come to ask me for advice in how they can earn a living. They find no other solution but to pour out their suffering before me—and thus do they find solace for their souls.... Anyone with eyes can see that the pain and suffering from all over the country comes to me—and this literally endangers my health....

Let no man travel here before revealing his troubles and needs before two or three prominent members of his community and if it is something that they can help with they should look into it well instead of rushing to write a letter of recommendation for him, as is the nature of our brotherhood who generally advise every troubled soul to go to Lubavitch etc....

If you must, send a letter with the individual to my brother or my son-in-law... who have agreed to be of help... My brother stood constantly before my father the Gaon of blessed memory, and it was through him that my father would provide answers and advice to all who asked in worldly matters for all the years that we were in Liadi, eleven years, as is known to our brotherhood. My brother's character is also common knowledge—and that he knows and understands all of our brotherhood and he can serve them with honesty and trustworthiness with his goodness, wisdom, and the goodness of his trustworthy heart....

Especially those who need [clarification] in words of Torah, should approach my son-in-law, Rabbi Menachem Mendel, who is at home in all chambers of Torah and spent much time serving my father the Gaon of blessed memory, even in spiritual matters, secret matters, matters between man and his fellow—and he can advise with the wisdom and fear of Heaven that is within him from his youth and from the abundance of good and upright [values] for every man that he received from my father the Gaon of blessed memory and from myself....

Yet despite the new rules, the Rebbe's health continued to deteriorate. His doctors advised him to visit and bathe in the hot springs. In the summer of 1825, he traveled to Carlsbad and remained there for the entire summer until he regained his health. He returned to his home for Sukkot of that year with new vigor and once again began to teach Chasidut. From all around Lubavith, chasidim came to be with their Rebbe for the festival of Sukkot, during which the Rebbe taught Chasidut in abundance.

* * *

On his way to Carlsbad, he met with the great Talmudist, Rabbi Akiva Eiger. He wrote of this trip in a letter to his son-in-law:

...In Posen I visited the Gaon and elder Rabbi Akiva Eiger. He is a guileless and upright man and knows nothing of the matters of this world. He wears a simple frock and a torn shtreimel. *He received us with great honor for he is modest, humble, and unassuming with all people.*

OPPOSITION

As if his poor health and the impoverished condition of his flock were not enough, the Rebbe was beset by bitter opponents. Just as his father had suffered opposition, the Mitteler Rebbe suffered the same.[23]

23. And like his father, the Rebbe suffered opposition from within the Chasidic camp as well.

Growing up, the Rebbe had a very close friend named Aharon. They were so close that a chasid once applied to them

During the Sukkot holiday of 1826, the chasidim found out that the Rebbe's opponents (from without) libeled him to the authorities, claiming that he intended to overthrow the government. They claimed that he had his shul built with the same dimensions as the Holy Temple and that he had raised enormous sums of money to topple the Czarist regime.

He was placed under arrest for over a month.

His imprisonment was benign when compared to his father's; he was allowed to teach Chasidut twice a week to a group of fifty chasidim. This concession was brought about through the efforts of Dr. Heibenthal, who insisted that teaching Chasidut was the Rebbe's life and sustenance—he needed to teach Chasidut just as an ordinary person needs food.

The Rebbe wrote a long letter to the Governor of Vitebsk, General Chavansky, in which he requests that "I wish to be judged by you… [since] your eyes will surely see what is true… more than any other governor or judge… to remove from me all false accusations." The Rebbe explained his request citing kabbalistic doctrine as explained in Chabad philosophy. This letter is published as a book called *Bad Kodesh* ("Holy Linen").

The Rebbe's request was received and he was indeed judged by General Chavansky.

During one session, the general insisted that the Rebbe and his antagonists have it out in his presence. In the midst of all the heated debate, one antagonist unwittingly called the Rebbe, *Rebbe*. The Rebbe picked up on this unconscious slip and said to the judge, "Look at this. Just a minute ago he said that I was a charlatan and a rebel—and now, he himself calls me *Rebbe*." The antagonist lost his composure and began speaking incoherently until the judge finally silenced him.

---

the Zoharic phrase *trein rayin d'lo misparshin*, two friends that never part. When the Alter Rebbe heard this he said: "*Halivai* (if only) they would never part."

As the Alter Rebbe had known, the two friends grew apart. Their methods of Divine worship contrasted sharply and a deep rift divided them. Rabbi Aharon established his own Chasidic court in Strashelye and thus became known as "Reb Aharon Strasheler."

Eventually, on the Ninth of Kislev, it was made known that the Rebbe was pronounced innocent and he was liberated on the next day, the 10th of Kislev. This day became a day of celebration for Chabad chasidim for all future generations. The Rebbe himself, however, would not have the chance to celebrate the anniversary of his liberation.

FINAL DAYS

In 1827, the Rebbe began hinting to the chasidim that his time had come. Once he said: "My father was fifty four years old when he was taken to Petersburg for the second time. He was then given the choice from Heaven to undergo suffering or to pass away—he chose suffering. It appears that he left the second option for me."

So it was. The Rebbe passed away at the age of fifty-four.

For Rosh Hashanah of 1827, the Rebbe traveled to his father's burial place in Haditch. After visiting his father's grave a number of times he said: "I prevailed upon my father to relieve me of my leadership role."

The chasidim who heard this assumed that the Rebbe intended to move to the Holy Land, something he had always yearned to do. They asked him how he could leave them "like sheep without a shepherd."

The Rebbe told them that his son-in-law, the Tzemach Tzedek would remain and serve them as a faithful leader.

From Haditch the Rebbe set out to Lubavitch by way of Niezhin. In Niezhin, he fell gravely ill and was forced to remain there. The greatest doctors were consulted but all of them said that they did not know of any cure for his illness. They warned him to refrain from teaching Chasidut. His illness grew worse each day and one could not even touch him, since he would immediately faint. So it went until the month of Kislev.

A week before his passing, the doctors were shocked that he was still alive. One of them said to the other: "I will show you something amazing. Now you see him lying there without any sign of life. But if we will merely allow him to speak Chasidic teachings he will arise as if newborn."

The doctors then allowed the Rebbe to teach Chasidut and he indeed arose, his face aglow. He began to speak about the forced conscription of Jewish young men into the Russian army that had recently been implemented. He said the following:

"I knew about this seven years ago, when I visited the grave of my father. I saw then a terrible decree upon the young men of Israel. My heart was broken within me for I understood and knew that this would occur eventually. Then, during the wedding of my daughter,[24] many wise and knowledgeable men, old and young, gathered to hear Chasidic teachings and I rejoiced greatly with them until the light of morning. I thought then that the decree had been annulled.

"Later, when I went to nap, my father came to me and said: 'What are you doing rejoicing with these lads that gathered to you? Do you not know of the decree that is gaining strength?'

"Immediately, my spirit was broken within me [for I knew that the decree] was about the conscription of Jewish lads."

He then proceeded to recite a chasidic discourse that began with the words "To understand the concept of the conscription of Jews as soldiers in the hands of foreigners...." The following is an excerpt from the discourse:

> *...Jews are placed in the hands of foreigners, who pass a razor over their beards and* payot *and force them to desecrate the Shabbos and many other prohibitions. And because of the physical pain that they inflict upon him his heart cries out to G-d with a bitter voice saying:*
>
> "'My G-d, my G-d, why have you forsaken me? Why are you far from my salvation and the words of my roar?' I was created only to fulfill Your will—I was not born for chaos and emptiness...."
>
> *...Although he is unable to fulfill many mitzvot, nev-*

24. According to the surmise of Rabbi Alexander Ziskind Pikarski, this refers to Rebbetzin Menucha Rachel, who married Rabbi Yakov Kuli. See his footnote to *Maamorei Admur Ha'emtzai, Kuntreisim*, p. 275.

ertheless the pain that he experiences because of the absence of those mitzvot is considered as if he had fulfilled them. He thereby sustains the entire world, as it is written 'and the tzaddik is the foundation of the world.'[25]

On the Eighth of Kislev, he instructed the chasidim to return to their homes and rejoice. The chasidim did not understand what the purpose of this rejoicing was and asked the Rebbe to clarify. He said: "Go and do as I told you. I will study the *Mishnah* of *Taharot*[26] and enjoy a bit."

On the night of Kislev 9, the Rebbe fainted numerous times. Each time, they roused him. The last time he fainted they were unable to bring him back. A great cry was heard in the home and word spread that the Rebbe was breathing his last. All the chasidim as well as the burial society gathered at the Rebbe's home. The burial society, seeing no sign of life, instructed the chasidim to stop the attempts at reviving him, since there was no longer any hope. The family and the chasidim did not pay them any attention. They approached the Rebbe and said: "Why does our master scare us so? Did he not hear the cry?"

The Rebbe responded: "I heard a voice call out: 'What does such a soul need in this world?'"

He then asked to be dressed in white. Redness returned to his face and he began to speak favorably of the Jewish people, saying that they are careful in the performance of *mitzvot*. He said that "although there is hatred and dissension among them—something that distressed me deeply throughout my life—at least they are extremely meticulous about the performance of *mitzvot*, especially the *mitzvah* of *tzedakah* in these difficult times, when each person gives more than his capacity."

After praying for mercy for his people, he instructed his family and the chasidim to be happy on that night, since joy "sweetens the judgments." He requested that the wise

25. See *Maamorei Admur Ha'emtzai, Kuntreisim*, p. 269.

26. A tractate of *Mishnah* dealing with the laws of Purity.

chasidim be summoned since he wished to deliver a chasidic discourse. The house was filled with light and joy—the chasidim were sure that the Rebbe would now return to good health.

The Rebbe expounded three times on the verse "*you shall walk after Your G-d*" and the verse "*the remembrance of your abundant goodness they will express.*" He said that "although the discourse has already been published in the Siddur, I will be your *melamed* and teach it to you with additional explanation." He taught with intense passion. A few times he asked whether the sun had risen—then, just before sunrise, he concluded his discourse with the words *for with you is the source of life from the life of life.*

As he concluded these words, his soul departed.

* * *

The Tzemach Tzedek later said: "Such a passing did not occur since the passing of Rabbi Shimon bar Yochai."[27]

The Rebbe passed away on the ninth of Kislev, 1827, fifty-four years after his birth—to the day. In him was fulfilled the blessing (Ex. 23:23): *I will fill the number of your days*—as the Talmud explains: *G-d fills the years of the righteous from day to day.*[28]

His resting place is in Niezhin.

---

27. Rabbi Shimon's final word was also "life."

28. *Rosh Hashanah* 11a. Similarly, Moses was born on the 7th of Adar and passed away on the same date.

IMPORTANT DATES

IMPORTANT DATES IN THE LIFE OF RABBI DOVBER OF LUBAVITCH

5534 (1773) Birth of Rabbi DovBer on Kislev 9.

5548 (1788) His marriage.

5550-51(1790-91) He is charged with guiding the younger Chasidim.

5573 (1813) In the month of Tevet, he accepts post of Rebbe. 18th Elul he settles in Lubavitch, Mogilev province.

5574 (1814) Appoints a special committee to reconstruct Jewish communities in White Russia that were destroyed during the war.

5575 (1815) Endeavors successfully to have government officials set aside tracts of land in Kherson province and establishes Jewish settlements there.

5576-7 (1816-7) Establishes settlement of Chabad Chasidim in Hebron, (Holy Land).

5577 (1817) Visits outlying settlements, and remains there from Pesach to Elul.

5587 (1826) Arrested because of slander, released on 10th Kislev. When the Czar's decree to conscript young Jews for military service becomes public knowledge, he travels to the grave of his father in Haditz. On Wednesday, 9 Kislev 5588 (1827) he passes away in Niezhin, Chernigov province, while returning from his father's gravesite, and is interred there.

His wife was Rebbetzin Sheina.

His sons:

1. Rabbi Menachem Nachum
2. Rabbi Baruch

His daughters:

1. Rebbetzin Sara, passed away in her youth.
2. Rebbetzin Beila. Her Husband: Rabbi Yekutiel Zalman.
3. Rebbetzin Chaya Mushka. Her Husband: Rabbi Menachem Mendel, the Tzemach Tzedek.
4. Rebbetzin Devorah Leah. Her Husband: Rabbi Yaakov Yisrael of Cherkass.
5. Rebbetzin Beracha. Her Husband: Rabbi Yonah.
6. Rebbetzin Menucha Rachel. Her Husband: Rabbi Yaakov Kuli Slonim.
7. Rebbetzin Sara. Her Husband: Rabbi Aaron Alexandrov of Shklov.

[8. Rebbetzin Esther Miriam]

PUBLISHED WORKS

PUBLISHED WORKS OF RABBI DOVBER

1. *Imrei Binah*
2. *Biurei Hazohar*
3. *Shaar Ha'emunah*
4. *Shaar Hayichud—bound with Shaar Ha'emunah*
5. *Shar Hateshuvah v'Hatefillah, 3 parts*
6. *Shaarei Orah*
7. *Derech Chaim*
8. *Ateret Rosh*
9. *Perush Hamilot*
10. *Hosafot l'Torah Or*
11. *Torat Chaim, Bereshit—Shemot*
12. *Mamarei Admur Ha'emtza'ee 18 vol.*
13. *Mamarei Admur Ha'emtza'ee, Hanachot 5577*
14. *Bad Kodesh*
15. *Maamar: B'Chaf Hey B'Kislev etc.*
16. *Maamar: Dor L'Dor*
17. *Maamar: L'Havin Inyan Kriat Yam Suf*
18. *Piskei Dinim—Yoreh Deah, Even Ha'ezer*
19. *Igrot Kodesh, 2 vol.*

OTHER TITLES IN
THE CHASIDIC HERITAGE SERIES

THE ETERNAL BOND *from Torah Or*

By Rabbi Schneur Zalman of Liadi
Translated by Rabbi Ari Sollish

This discourse explores the spiritual significance of *brit milah*, analyzing two dimensions in which our connection with G-d may be realized. For in truth, there are two forms of spiritual circumcision: Initially, man must "circumcise his heart," freeing himself to the best of his ability from his negative, physical drives; ultimately, though, it is G-d who truly liberates man from his material attachment.

JOURNEY OF THE SOUL from *Torah Or*

By Rabbi Schneur Zalman of Liadi
Translated by Rabbi Ari Sollish

Drawing upon the parallel between Queen Esther's impassioned plea to King Ahasuerus for salvation and the soul's entreaty to G-d for help in its spiritual struggle, this discourse examines the root of the soul's exile, and the dynamics by which it lifts itself from the grip of materiality and ultimately finds a voice with which to express its G-dly yearnings. Includes a brief biography of the author.

TRANSFORMING THE INNER SELF from *Likkutei Torah*

By Rabbi Schneur Zalman of Liadi
Translated by Rabbi Ari Sollish

This discourse presents a modern-day perspective on the Biblical command to offer animal sacrifices. Rabbi Schneur Zalman teaches that each of us possesses certain character traits that can be seen as "animalistic," or materialistic, in nature, which can lead a person toward a life of material indulgence. Our charge, then, is to "sacrifice" and transform the animal within, to refine our animal traits and utilize them in our pursuit of spiritual perfection.

FLAMES from *Gates of Radiance*

By Rabbi DovBer of Lubavitch
Translated by Dr. Naftoli Loewenthal

This discourse focuses on the multiple images of the lamp, the oil, the wick and the different hues of the flame in order to express profound guidance in the divine service of every individual. Although *Flames* is a Chanukah discourse, at the same time, it presents concepts that are of perennial significance. Includes the first English biography of the author ever published.

THE MITZVAH TO LOVE YOUR FELLOW AS YOURSELF from *Derech Mitzvotecha*

By Rabbi Menachem Mendel of Lubavitch, the Tzemach Tzedek
Translated by Rabbis Nissan Mangel and Zalman Posner

The discourse discusses the Kabbalistic principle of the "collective soul of the world of *Tikkun*" and explores the essential unity of all souls. The discourse develops the idea that when we connect on a soul level, we can love our fellow as we love ourselves; for in truth, we are all one soul. Includes a brief biography of the author.

TRUE EXISTENCE *Mi Chamocha 5629*

By Rabbi Shmuel of Lubavitch
Translated by Rabbis Yosef Marcus and Avraham D. Vaisfiche

This discourse revolutionizes the age-old notion of Monotheism, i.e., that there is no other god besides Him. Culling from Talmudic and Midrashic sources, the discourse makes the case that not only is there no other god besides Him, there is nothing besides Him—literally. The only thing that truly exists is G-d. Includes a brief biography of the author.

TRUE EXISTENCE *The Chasidic View of Reality*

A Video-CD with Rabbi Manis Friedman

Venture beyond science and Kabbalah and discover the world of Chasidism. This Video-CD takes the viewer step-by-step through the basic chasidic and kabbalistic view of creation and existence. In clear, lucid language, Rabbi Manis Friedman deciphers these esoteric concepts and demonstrates their modern-day applications.

YOM TOV SHEL ROSH HASHANAH 5659

Discourse One

By Rabbi Shalom DovBer of Lubavitch

Translated by Rabbis Yosef Marcus and Moshe Miller

The discourse explores the attribute of *malchut* and the power of speech while introducing some of the basic concepts of Chasidism and Kabbalah in a relatively easy to follow format. Despite its title and date of inception, the discourse is germane throughout the year. Includes a brief biography of the author.

FORCES IN CREATION

Yom Tov Shel Rosh Hashanah 5659 Discourse Two

By Rabbi Shalom DovBer of Lubavitch

Translated by Rabbis Moshe Miller and Shmuel Marcus

This is a fascinating journey beyond the terrestrial, into the myriad spiritual realms that shape our existence. In this discourse, Rabbi Shalom DovBer systematically traces the origins of earth, Torah and souls, drawing the reader higher and higher into the mystical, cosmic dimensions that lie beyond the here and now, and granting a deeper awareness of who we are at our core.

THE PRINCIPLES OF EDUCATION AND GUIDANCE

Klalei Hachinuch Vehahadrachah

By Rabbi Yosef Yitzchak of Lubavitch

Translated by Rabbi Y. Eliezer Danzinger

The Principles of Education and Guidance is a compelling treatise that examines the art of educating. In this thought provoking analysis, Rabbi Yosef Yitzchak teaches how to assess the potential of any pupil, how to objectively evaluate one's own strengths, and how to successfully use reward and punishment—methods that will help one become a more effective educator.

THE FOUR WORLDS

By Rabbi Yosef Yitzchak of Lubavitch

Translated by Rabbis Yosef Marcus and Avraham D. Vaisfiche

Overview by Rabbi J. Immanuel Schochet

At the core of our identity is the desire to be one with our source, and to know the spiritual realities that give our physical life the transcendental importance of the Torah's imperatives. In this letter to a yearning Chasid, the Rebbe explains the mystical worlds of Atzilut, Beriah, Yetzira, and Asiya.

ONENESS IN CREATION

By Rabbi Yosef Yitzchak of Lubavitch

Translated by Rabbi Y. Eliezer Danzinger

Said by Rabbi Yosef Yitzchak at the close of his 1930 visit to Chicago, this discourse explores the concept of Divine Unity as expressed in the first verse of the Shema. The discourse maintains that it is a G-dly force that perpetually sustains all of creation. As such, G-d is one with creation. And it is our study of Torah and performance of the mitzvot that reveals this essential oneness.

GARMENTS OF THE SOUL

Vayishlach Yehoshua 5736

By Rabbi Menachem M. Schneerson, the Lubavitcher Rebbe
Translated by Rabbi Yosef Marcus

Often what is perceived in this world as secondary is in reality most sublime. What appears to be mundane and inconsequential is often most sacred and crucial. Thus at their source, the garments of the human, both physical and spiritual, transcend the individual.

THE UNBREAKABLE SOUL

Mayim Rabbim 5738

By Rabbi Menachem M. Schneerson, the Lubavitcher Rebbe
Translated by Rabbi Ari Sollish

The discourse begins with an unequivocal declaration: No matter how much one may be inundated with materialism, the flame of the soul burns forever. This discourse speaks to one who finds pleasure in the material world, yet struggles to find spirituality in his or her life.

ON THE ESSENCE OF CHASIDUS

Kunteres Inyana Shel Toras Hachasidus

By Rabbi Menachem M. Schneerson, the Lubavitcher Rebbe

In this landmark discourse, the Lubavitcher Rebbe, Rabbi Menachem M. Schneerson, explores the contribution of Chasidus to a far deeper and expanded understanding of Torah. The Rebbe analyzes the relationship Chasidus has with Kabbalah, the various dimensions of the soul, the concept of Moshiach and the Divine attributes—all in this slim volume.

COMING SOON!

YOM TOV SHEL ROSH HASHANAH 5659

Discourse Three

By Rabbi Shalom DovBer of Lubavitch

Translated by Rabbi Y. Eliezer Danzinger

HACHODESH 5700

By Rabbi Yosef Yitzchak of Lubavitch

Translated by Rabbi Yosef Marcus

VE'ATAH TETZAVEH 5741

By Rabbi Menachem M. Schneerson, the Lubavitcher Rebbe

Translated by Rabbi Yosef Marcus

הוצאת ספרים
קרני הוד תורה
קה"ת
ליובאוויטש